LONDON

WAS

YESTERDAY

LONDON WAS YESTERDAY

1934–1939
Janet Flanner

Edited by Irving Drutman

A Studio Book · The Viking Press · New York

Prefatory Note

The material in this volume originally appeared in *The New Yorker*, all of it (except for the Profile of Queen Mary) under the heading "Letter from London." During the period covered—1934 until the outbreak of war in September 1939—Janet Flanner continued as well to write her fortnightly Paris Letter, the reports from both capitals appearing over her *nom de correspondance, Genêt*.

The comments in bold type accompanying the photographs are her current reflections on London notables of the decade.

I.D.

Frontispiece: A Grenadier guardsman approaching the gates of Buckingham Palace, which proudly display the Royal coat of arms.

Introduction

One of the charms of London is that it seems to be the home of habit. History has settled there quietly. The odd alternatives in modesty and ostentation that especially mark its central neighborhoods are nowhere more clearly demonstrated than in the panoramic sweep, beside the Thames, of the Gothic Houses of Parliament, and the nearby unassuming brick residence, one of a row four stories high, of the Prime Minister, Great Britain's most important government functionary, at Number 10 Downing Street. The permanent official address of England's dominant political brain, Number 10 is marked by neither symbol nor inscription to distinguish it from its unexceptional neighbors, with which it is identical. An address famous around the world is made conspicuous only by an ordinary street lamp hung over its entrance.

London is a great metropolis, crowded with people, all of them living courteously crammed together. After generations of practice, English life has become highly classified, one class rubbing against the next with a minimum of abrasion. One cannot easily think of any other nation whose upper classes have benefited more, have had more pleasure from being what they are—high born, well educated, and usually rich—with town houses and ample country places in which to carry on their habit of a balanced, civilized existence, partly metropolitan, partly rural, for habitual weekends. Though their middle class is as conventional as that of most other countries, the British working class is unique: it has a flavor, a pungency all its own.

As a foreigner, my first intimate experience with this class began when, arriving from Paris in the spring of 1934, I took a taxi from Victoria Station to an address that had been recommended in Clarges Street, near Shepherd's Market. Here I rented a flat—bedroom, sitting room, and bath—in a house operated by an ex-butler named McCulloch and his portly Irish wife. To help build up the family income, Mrs. McCulloch would serve simple meals upon request, and it soon got so that many of us in the house would eat nowhere else. Her creamed haddock was a dream. Since I can't cook at all, I once asked her, as I watched her stirring the milk in the pan, "How do you know when it's done?" She said, "I just keep tasting it until it's good enough for Mr. McCulloch and me." That seemed to me a very sensible idea for regulating a recipe. It's done when it tastes good enough.

The McCullochs had two darling daughters, both pretty. One was apprenticed to the smartest hairdresser in the center of Mayfair and the other to a luxury milliner. The girls' manners and accents seemed to me to be impeccable imitations of those of the upper middle class, unlike the speech of their parents, which placed the latter indelibly in the serving class.

5

I was horrified one day when by chance I saw the confined space into which this family of four was crowded in the basement of the house—and so quiet, never a peep out of them. When someone once asked, "How do the McCullochs live?" I said truthfully, "Like mice," a phrase that for some reason became a household synonym for cramped quarters to all my friends who came to stay there.

James Thurber and his wife, Helen, moved in for a short time, at my recommendation, and I well remember the night Thurber kept ordering drink after drink from McCulloch, each time insisting that McCulloch join him in one more, until they were both so pickled in alcohol that I had to go down to the kitchen to replenish the ice bucket, McCulloch no longer being able to negotiate the stairs. Finally the three females, Helen, Mrs. McCulloch, and I, managed to get the two gentlemen to their beds, and I was solemnly thanked the next morning by a bleary-eyed McCulloch for "helping" Mrs. McCulloch with her duties (which of course were his, not hers) the night before.

I was living it seems in the heart of the high-class London prostitute district—"writers and prostitutes" is the way a Paris friend categorized the inhabitants of the area. I knew some of the writers, and the girls standing on the street corners soon got to know me. As I passed them on the way home in the early evening, they would snarl a greeting at me. I still don't understand why; it is inconceivable to me that they could have thought of an American woman so bourgeois in appearance as I was as competition. My male British friends told me that the tarts in the neighborhood all worked for a syndicate, which supplied their clothes. Remarkable clothes they were, too. If a girl wore a purple suit, she wore purple shoes, with all other accessories to match. When the syndicate felt the costumes had seen enough duty in Mayfair, it passed them on to the next lower category working in a less affluent district that it also controlled. The only other city in which I had observed such institutionalized prostitution was in the Berlin of the 1920s (where the girls idiosyncratically wore different types of the then newly popular sports clothes, some being garbed in ski trousers and going so far as to carry skis, which must have been an encumbrance in the exercise of their profession).

I knew some English people in Paris but very few on their home grounds. One of these Paris friends was Madge Garland, for years fashion editor of the British *Vogue,* who liked Americans and kindly piloted me around to London tea parties to meet various people whose houses she frequented. I am not a good intruder, but Madge would steer me very skillfully so that I could be introduced to all the more interesting characters in a room.

To this day I am especially grateful to her for having taken me to tea with the gifted eccentric writer Ivy Compton-Burnett, a distinctive Victorian personality whose novels were all on the same pattern, as alike as two peas and as delicious. All of these novels contained similar casts of characters from the landed gentry: father or stepfather, mother or stepmother, precocious offspring and precocious servants, each family unit leading seemingly conventional, though in fact highly disturbed, country lives, with domestic lapses toward incest, murder, or the forging of wills; one of her novels so much like the other that it was difficult to remember which one had been read and which one was looking forward to reading with equal pleasure. The acute,

"... the panoramic sweep, beside the Thames, of the Gothic
Houses of Parliament...."

dazzling talk erupting on her pages was a manual of evasive upper-class British conversation, although her own talk over tea—with scrupulous intensity she sat in a chair close to me in a sort of concentrated hospitality—inclined toward the prosaic. As I discovered, what she loved to dwell on conversationally was on things to eat, especially cakes.

Another English friend I knew from Paris was the landscape gardener Russell Page. There are two things I especially connect with Russell. One was a wonderful old aunt of his from Wiltshire whom he and I called, behind her back, Red Stockings, because she always wore them, having knitted them herself out of silk. She would turn up about once a fortnight in a hired car to take Russell and a friend or so, usually me, driving around the countryside, with no particular destination in mind. Just driving and just looking. He also had two well-known gardening friends, one, a woman so famous in her profession that an artist had actually painted a portrait of her gardening shoes; the other, a man who was acclaimed for the special varieties and colors of delphiniums he had recently developed. If you didn't have those in your garden, you might just as well have planted dandelions.

Harold Ross, editor of *The New Yorker*, had asked me to undertake a "Letter from London," to alternate with my fortnightly Paris Letter. He had also assigned me to write a Profile of the then-reigning Queen Mary, the basic material to be supplied upon request, as was customary, by the press officer of Buckingham Palace. However for the added little personal touches which I felt were necessary to make the Profile more entertaining, I would 7

Nancy Cunard.

Nancy was extraordinary looking, eccentric, gifted—one of the best modern English poets—prototype for the leading female figure in two celebrated novels of the 1920s, Aldous Huxley's *roman à clef*, Point Counter Point, and Michael Arlen's audacious The Green Hat. Nancy's mother the California-born Lady Emerald Cunard was one of a trio (along with Margot Asquith and Lady Sybil Colefax) of energetic, celebrity-hungry London hostesses prominent in the Edward VIII–Wallis Simpson circle. Nancy enjoyed a perpetual feud with her mother. While still young, she once hopefully asked Emerald's intimate friend and admirer, the novelist George Moore, if there was any possibility that he might be her father. "Oh my dear," answered this 1890s reprobate, "that's a question a little girl should ask of her mother"—to whom, of course as usual, she wasn't speaking. Once when I was going to London for an extended period, Nancy made me promise never to be introduced to Lady Cunard. "Besides," she added defensively, "you might like her."

have to forage around for myself. Luckily, a great deal of accurate floating information about the Queen was available, stored as gossip among the titled classes. Lady Juliet Duff, whom I had known in Paris, and was very fond of, was especially useful. She introduced me to many noblewomen who were willing to talk extra freely when they knew that I was writing for a responsible magazine about their dear Queen.

Lady Juliet was one of the outstanding personalities of London. Her father had been Lord Lonsdale, brother of the famous "sporting earl"; her mother, upon a second marriage to the Marquis of Ripon, became, as the Marchioness, a noted Edwardian hostess and the great patroness of Diaghilev. Lady Juliet's fortune was derived from slate quarries that her family had owned for generations. The daughter was as distinguished as her mother. Certainly there was nothing average about Lady Juliet. She was six-foot tall, dressed smartly, was intelligent, and was excellent company. She kept up with London gossip as if it were a matter of immediate history. Her intimates were the beautiful social butterfly Lady Diana Cooper, the Lunts, Noël Coward and Ivor Novello (she was extremely stage struck), the writers Hilaire Belloc, Maurice Baring, Anthony Powell, and the diplomat-writer Harold Nicolson. Thursdays, as a rule, Winston Churchill would come over to play piquet with her. She knew everyone in Court circles, which considered her a bit bohemian. She was quite internationalized and was acquainted with many Americans; she had been vetted by them and knew how to take them. I found all the English men who were part of her entourage amusing, even when they were being serious.

Lady Juliet had an extensive house in the country, near Salisbury, to which she was kind enough to invite me for occasional weekends. Knowing my passion for steak and kidney pie, she always served her cook's special version of this great dish, with oysters in it, the whole steamed in a tall white crock. I also remember how impressed I was by a magnificent tree, some sort of conifer, on Juliet's front lawn, by legend one of those trees planted by James the Old Pretender, which meant that that house had been up even longer than it looked to my alien eyes.

Sometimes we went to visit a neighbor who had a cottage on the local river, an area dominated by several families of belligerent swans. These majestic birds, fiends in feathered form, were the enemies of all the small terriers who lived by the waterside and who invariably barked at them. The little dogs were perhaps clever but not very prudent. As the swans swam proudly by, close to shore, one would reach out, grab a yapping dog by the throat and duck him until he drowned. The mortality among terriers during a summer could be quite high. Also in the neighborhood was a family named Pepys, remote descendants of the famous diarist. When, with an apology, I asked the head of the house how they pronounced their name, he briskly replied, "Exactly as it is spelled." When I told him that in the United States we had been taught to pronounce it "peeps," he roared with laughter and said that nothing could be more ludicrous. Pepys, then, I suppose it is—duo-syllabic and as spelled.

Lady Juliet Duff.

Sir Alfred Duff Cooper and "the beautiful social butterfly Lady Diana Cooper. . . ."

Juliet and her circle's invaluable trivia about Queen Mary proved to be of great help. I also obtained some characteristic sidelights on the Queen from several of the Royal tradespeople. One of Her Majesty's minor dressmakers told me, and as someone who is impatient about ordering clothes it particularly interested me because it seemed so sensible, about the Queen's system for choosing her everyday, as opposed to her State, wardrobe. The dressmaker would arrive by appointment at Buckingham Palace with several suitcases full of garments which she thought might suit the Queen's taste, and the King's taste, too, since his approbation was very important to the Queen, and they were both against any excessive prevailing fashions. In Her Majesty's apartment, the dressmaker and her young assistant would unpack the suits and gowns, and the Queen, instead of trying them on, would stand in front of a pier glass and hold them up in front of her, stretching each candidate across the Royal bosom. Those that both she and the King liked would be put in one heap, and the discards in another. Not much important Royal time wasted.

From the young Duke of Kent, through his friend and mine, the novelist Louis Bromfield, I received a charming anecdote about the Queen. It seems

Queen Mary joins in line with a group of nursery-school children.

Their Majesties on holiday with their daughter-in-law the
Duchess of York and granddaughter Princess Elizabeth.

that somewhere in Buckingham Palace, in an Oriental room, there is a row
of tall Buddhas whose heads rest on articulated necks which permit them if
touched to nod up and down. The Duke passed by this room early one day
as the Queen, unaware of his presence, was walking through. To his astonish-
ment and amusement he saw his mother pause as she approached each figure
and gently tap its head, sending the row nodding. A mandatory morning
salute, as near as he could make out.

The Profile must have been to the point because, shortly after it was
published, Louis told me he had a message for me from the Duke of Kent:
"Tell your friend Miss Flanner that all of us boys thought it was a very good
portrait of Mamma and often just like her. We were especially glad that she
mentioned Mamma's overly large hats, against which we are powerless."

The decade is notable in British royal history for the fact that within
a space of one year it featured three reigning monarchs. George V died on
January 20, 1936, to be succeeded by his eldest son, Edward VIII, who abdi-
cated his throne on December 11 of the same year, in a tumultuous melodra-
matic renunciation, to marry the American divorcee Mrs. Wallis Simpson—
who would ever have thought such things could happen?—to be succeeded
in turn by his younger brother George VI. The Crisis, as the stages leading
up to the Abdication came to be called, was the most spectacular domestic
event that England had known in modern times and at one point, as it was
approaching its startling denouement, temporarily threatened to tear the
country apart. Feelings ran very high. Anything American was automatically
unpopular.

Edward's liaison with Mrs. Simpson was familiar gossip in the higher reaches of London society. It had been obliquely and increasingly mentioned in the foreign press but with ostentatious tact had been completely ignored by the British newspapers. When the culminating weight of the affair became uncontrollable and near to explosion, *The New Yorker* cabled me asking if I could do a character sketch of Mrs. Simpson, of whom after all very little was known to the general public—and also to me. An old friend of mine, Main Bocher, who designed most of Mrs. Simpson's clothes, kindly supplied me with useful, casual but acute observations he had made on her psychology and individuality, and several London friends of hers also furnished basic details of her daily habits. This cursory study of Mrs. Simpson could not have been amiss, since after the Crisis had been turned into conjugal history by her marriage to the ex-King in a borrowed French château, she wrote an appreciative letter to *The New Yorker*'s editor thanking him for the courteous, intelligent, and unmalicious treatment—a novelty for that hectored woman at the time—that she had received in the magazine. Ross was so pleased with the letter that he had it framed and hung on the wall of his office, where it remained for years. It was always a source of exasperation to me that although it was I who had written the articles which had elicited the letter, I was never offered possession of it. I wonder where that letter is today.

On the tense day of the Abdication itself, I was lunching at the Ritz, as was everyone else. Many of those present had somehow become privy to the contents of the Abdication radio speech which King Edward was to deliver that afternoon to Parliament and were quoting its most important negating phrase, "without the woman I love." A luncheon party at a table near me included, among others, Victor Cunard (who later told me about the conversation) and the venerable Mrs. Keppel, the favorite and unsanctified relict of the departing King's grandfather Edward VII. It seems that the peak remark at their table, or indeed at any table in the whole room, had a consensus been taken, consisted of Mrs. Keppel's devasting observation, "Things were done better in *my* day."

In the line of duty and also pleasure, I always attended whatever I considered notable in the world of theatre, ballet, and opera. During the seasons I was regularly there, the most stimulating theatrical performances in London were those given at the Old Vic by the Shakespeare Repertory Company, then I believe under the management of Tyrone Guthrie. I particularly recall the splendid Hamlets of Laurence Olivier and Alec Guinness—no less impressive, to my mind, than the beautifully spoken, choreographic Hamlet of John Gielgud—and Emlyn Williams' chilling Gloucester in *Richard III*. Of the many outstanding dance performances I witnessed, I fear that the most memorable was an evening of *Swan Lake* by the Vic-Wells ballet during a minor smallpox epidemic in the city, when every pretty little cygnet appeared with a pretty little plaster on her arm to cover her vaccination. There was also a most upsetting evening at Covent Garden when Lotte Lehmann, performing her most famous role, the Marschallin in *Der Rosenkavalier*, suddenly stopped singing toward the close of Act One—after the phrase *"drin ist die silberne Rose"*—and with an agonized appeal to the audience, said in English, "Oh, I can't go on," following which she rushed off the stage. Sir Thomas Beecham, who was directing the orchestra, quietly brought it to a halt. There was at first complete silence in the auditorium, then a well-bred buzz. The manners of the British audience were impeccable; in Paris, I am afraid, there would have been an outbreak of catcalls and whistles. After a short interval, we were informed by a stage announcement that Hilde Konetzni, an Austrian singer who until a few moments before had been sitting in a box, would continue in the role.

The remainder of what went on behind the curtain I learned later from Olga Lynn, a well-known musician and friend of mine who was an avid and accurate gossip. Olga had rushed backstage shortly after Lotte Lehmann's anguished outcry and disappearance, in time to see the wardrobe mistress slit the Marschallin's costume down the back (since the substitute singer was heavier than Frau Lehmann) tape across the opening, and improvise a cape to cover the discrepancy. Mme. Konetzni was then ready to continue, with her rather rasping voice, in the dulcet Lehmann's role. The public report was that Lehmann had "suffered an indisposition" after a very bad sea crossing, but Olga told me that the reason for Lehmann's *défaillance* had been

Noël Coward with the Duke and Duchess of Kent.

"I particularly recall the splendid Hamlets of Laurence Olivier [*right*] and Alec Guinness—no less impressive, to my mind, than the beautifully spoken, choreographic Hamlet of John Gielgud [*left*]—and [*above*] Emlyn Williams' chilling Gloucester in *Richard III*."

that she had received word just before stepping on stage that the Jewish children of her husband had been seized in Vienna by the Nazis.

This was in May 1938, two months after the German annexation of Austria. In September the umbrella-toting, obstinately nonbelligerent Prime Minister Neville Chamberlain returned from the Munich "appeasement" conference which sacrificed Czechoslovakia; his stop-gap "peace in our time" slogan quieted the English public's apprehensions for the moment. A state of worried suspension lasted until early September of the following year when Germany marched into Poland. England and France then reluctantly declared war on September 3, 1939. It had come after all.

During the war years, which I had perforce to spend in New York, I received no word of my English friends. When I returned to London in late 1944, en route to the recently liberated Paris, I went with natural curiosity to what had been the McCullochs' address on Clarges Street. The house had totally disappeared. Where it had been there was now one vast hole filled with water. Its emplacement had been turned into a reservoir to quench incendiary fires in the neighborhood caused by the itinerant buzz bombs the Germans were desperately sending over as their last resort. Neighbors whom I questioned said the house had received a direct hit. Fortunately the McCullochs, I was told, were at the seashore at the time.

Alas, that casual domestic world we had known together in Clarges Street was not to be reconstituted. My former landlord and his family had disappeared into the depths of England and I never heard from them again.

Janet Flanner

Debutantes arriving in the Mall for presentation to Their Majesties at Buckingham Palace.

Londen is enjoying two novel states. It is sunny enough to have produced a rare water shortage; it has money enough to have created an even rarer Season. For over a year, business in England has been taking a profit; for less than a year it has been spending it. Their Majesties' Courts at Buckingham Palace are providing a climax for both. Four Courts are being held this year: two in May, two in pre-Ascot June. About six hundred ladies a night, or, if you prefer, a total of twenty-four hundred females in feathers, are being presented. Around their curtsies, the customs of thousands of aristocrats and the commerce of millions of tradesmen rise in prosperous mutual motion. For England's budget is balanced, and with a surplus; sixpence is off the income tax. It is good news for any capital that the Empire's capital is again having good times.

1934

The protocol governing these Court-presentation costumes is perhaps the last strict social ruling on a lawless, changing earth. From Madame Elspeth Champcommunal of W. W. Reville-Terry, which, after generations of Court and Queen dressmaking, probably knows more about trains and feathers than anybody else except the Lord Chamberlain, come the following immutable facts: The King and Queen want gowns low and long, regardless of fashion; last year, stylish high-fronted numbers appeared. The King didn't like that. The Prince of Wales's three white ostrich feathers, plus a twenty-seven-inch white veil, must be placed on the head in the *Ich Dien* motto manner; are an order, not an ornament; are often handed down from duchess to grandchild the worse for wear; and may, by special permission, be three black ostrich feathers in the case of a widow. The 1934 trains stretch eighteen inches back from the heel, are *manteaux de cour*, were four and a half yards long before the war, were cut off entirely in postwar 1919, and the following year cut down to the present two and a half yards from the shoulder. (The extra-long queues of *nouveaux riches*, plus their fourteen-foot trains, were apparently more than the Queen could stand.) At Reville-Terry, the train's weight is distributed between shoulder hooks and stocking tops by a special net corselet, with garters, to prevent the gown from pulling back, or even off. Rehearsal of gown, shoes, feathers, fan, jewels, and curtsy are held in the shop before the gown is delivered. Jewels are a great problem in Court-dress designing when fine family stones form the front of the frock. Court gowns must be flamboyant to show against the Palace gilt, the Queen's blaze of diamonds, and the Royal Household uniforms; a mere chic Paris frock would stand no chance in Buckingham. Before entry to the Throne Room, trains are settled in place by attendants with long ivory poles. Curtsies have from time immemorial been taught by Miss Vacani; Truefitt or Douglas of Bond Street are still the hieratic hairdressers. A debutante is presented by her mother; after marriage, is re-presented by her mother-in-law. Court begins at 9:30 p.m. and ends around midnight, with supper after, the King's catering being done by Lyons, the teashop people, and very good.

This year's limousines and men-on-box are again seen, both cars and servants in old family coach and livery colors. Last year, motors of ladies Court-bound were for the first time allowed immediate entry into the palace yard rather than kept waiting hours on the Mall—perhaps to relieve them of being admired by the unemployed. At any rate, this year's unemployed have nothing to look at on Court nights at all.

Spotlights brighten the Royal Box during a command performance at the Palladium Music Hall.

Recent by-elections are returning not a few Labour candidates. It may be that this year's rush to Court presupposes a next year's Labour government.

In the meantime there are great balls nightly in great houses, plus champagne, and there were nineteen theatre first nights in one week—all sights lately unseen—as well as two fashionable movie first nights, something no one here had ever laid eyes on before. Indeed, the world première of *The Scarlet Empress* was as much a triumph for debutantes as it was a failure for Dietrich. Even more *rarissime* was the Tivoli movie theatre's first night of *The House of Rothschild*, which was attended by the house of Rothschild—Mrs. Anthony de Rothschild, Mrs. Leopold de Rothschild, Baroness Alphonse Rothschild, Miss Rosemary de Rothschild, and Liberty Rothschild. Considering how the family figure in the film, lots of people and papers thought not only that they shouldn't have turned up (even if it was British-given for German-Jewish charity) but also that they should have discouraged others from turning up by suppressing the film, as their French cousins did in Paris. Furthermore, up to the moment of the Hollywood production, London still thought Waterloo had been won on the playing fields of Eton, or anyhow by Wellington. Without necessarily believing it, the town saw the victory as gained on a counting table and by a man from Frankfurt.

Though the Season's American contingent of plays—*Biography, Counsellor-at-Law, Reunion in Vienna,* etc.—were not ten-strikes, and though actual money was lost on Gaston Baty's Paris troupe, and the Comédie-Française's Victor Hugo evenings passed in diplomatic silence, London's new theatrical love is a foreigner. For London is now crazy about Elisabeth Bergner. Critics must have been lunatic to compare her to Bernhardt and Duse; she is a great deal like Laurette Taylor. Her Margaret Kennedy play, *Escape Me Never*, is a continuation of the *Constant Nymph* Sanger family saga, and no play, though if produced in Britain rather than in Hollywood it might be a movie. Apparently, Miss Bergner wrote the last act, which should be a load off Miss Kennedy's conscience. Miss Bergner now has lovely orange hair (it was brown in Germany), which she scratches constantly; the body of a boy of ten, a not very pleasant *hinter*-Berlin British voice, and is still an excellently trained, highly talented character actress of thirty-odd years. She has always been more an exceptional depository for personality than a regular artist. She should, and deservedly, repeat her London hit next autumn in New York,* or indeed anywhere.

* She did, for a highly successful run of twelve weeks, at New York's Shubert Theatre.

"London's new theatrical love is a foreigner. For London is now crazy about Elisabeth Bergner." A scene from *Escape Me Never*.

Covent Garden is like no other opera house for sweetly gaudy gilt, footstools, drafts, and a ladies' retiring room to which ladies really retire to ruff their hair, remove sweaters, straighten diamond tiaras, etc. This year, at the opening of the International Opera Season, it was also like no other theatre for shock—aroused when Sir Thomas Beecham, who was conducting, shouted at chattering people to Keep Still. The other great item of its program— unfortunately less appreciated by Londoners—was Strauss's new *Arabella*, which contained golden, sensuous thefts from *Salome* and *Rosenkavalier*, and a divine Act One duet and Act Three introduction. Buying records of it is an inexpensive way of proving the Londoners wrong.

Ink can't describe this year's annual Royal Tournament at Olympia. Such a superb three-hour military circus of bands, cavalrymen (dressed as Picasso harlequins and Degas chorines), naval rope-climbers, Air Force acrobats, musical drives, and leopard-skinned drummers, all under a blue-chiffoned glass roof against a British twilight sky, demands eyes, ears, and a front seat to be fully appreciated. People who had never had enough of kilts and bagpipes finally had sufficient of both in the Second Battalion of the Black Watch's lengthy pageant enacting, with wigs, costumes, and dialogue, its musical history from 1745 (piping "The Black Highland Laddie") to 1934 ("Blue Bonnets Over the Border," with extra-fancy thumps from the skirted drummers). Even pacifists can enjoy such a ballet. With their plaid petticoats, white spats, pendulum arms, and windy band, these myriad Scotchmen looked as graceful and peaceful as men in a great dance.

Covent Garden Opera House.

Four times during the Silver Jubilee, which opens officially next Monday to celebrate the twenty-fifth year of the present Georgian reign, Her Majesty the Queen of England will drive in state by His Majesty the King's side toward the four points of the compass—east, west, north, south—through the capital city of London. And from all directions from all over the Empire, people will have assembled, having come over water, mountains, veldts, moors, hot plains, to meet together on the curb, in the club, in windows, on grandstands, and rooftops, to see the sight go by. After months of preparation, after hours of waiting, for one moment they will see the faces of a man and of a taller woman.

It is possible that today nobody knows what the Queen of England is really like, not even the Queen. For twenty-five years she has given twelve to eighteen hours of her days, and the total of her energy and conscience, to not being herself. She was born with a full lower lip and a high temper, only one of which is still visible. In her career she has been limited to her native good qualities, which are all she has had a chance to develop. The result is her fine photogenic façade, a splendid surface which she has, in the face of the peculiar privations of royalty, erected and ornamented in a quarter-century's labor and on which nothing private now shows. Even for those to whom the privilege is open, she is hard to get to know, and she is always a surprise to new friends. She has no small talk. As a debutante, she already refused to say what everyone knew about the English weather. In general conversation she probably gets along best with men, since she was an only and elder sister to three brothers; she also has borne five sons. England is a man's island and she is its Queen. Flattery alarms her—she wants nothing beyond brief appreciation; she likes the sensible statement and gives it, can't make a speech but knows how to speak her mind, and gets to the point without shilly-shally, since she has no patience with waste in any form. She has the habit of generosity but is by nature saving; when she was a child, her parents, the Tecks, were poor. She never dawdles about coming to a decision. Common sense is corporate in her comment or advice on any topic; the Ladies of her Household consider her a sound judge in any ticklish situation and a comfort in grief, which, since she is related to nearly every royal family in Europe, she has in past years become fatally familiar with. In her friendships, the Queen is thoughtful and inventive rather than emotional and imaginative. Only her family connections call her May. No one else calls her Mary. She is shy, which has been a great drawback to her, especially during the early, trying years of her reign; as a shy child, she constantly melted into tears (she sobbed at her first sight of Queen Victoria); as a shy grandmother, her straight back and face still stiffen occasionally. Whatever it may cost her to be stared at annually by millions and to meet thousands, she now uses a priceless stateliness to cover her discomfiture. Her smile to the crowds is neither frequent nor facile, but her bow gives great satisfaction to her subjects. Graciousness has come to be as much of her public style as of any actress's, except that the Queen has no histrionics. She has merely a crown, qualities, courage, discipline, and, no matter what the calendar says, the nineteenth century to lean upon. She is perpetually polite, though as a little girl she used to have the relief of what her contemporaries called "flaring up"—but that was long ago.

Good health and general interest are her two vital mainsprings: in her long Queenship, she's had nothing worse than a couple of bad colds; her curiosity is intense and she loves information—a habit of mind that is often a trial to institution officials, but she gets the information. When she goes to visit a private house for the first time, she invariably asks to see it from top to bottom. This leads to a lot of extemporaneous cleaning when the Queen is coming, especially in the kitchen regions, for she has a domestic passion for modern sanitation, labor-saving devices, and storerooms.

She is not a gardening fiend but a flower addict, favoring cut carnations in the tenderer colors, especially pink, and hydrangeas. Maybe because the English have spent her life saying she is typically English, the Queen has less taste in music than she would have had had her Teck father remained in Germany. Her favorite operas are *Madame Butterfly* and *La Bohème;* she makes no excuses—she is interested in other things. She is only a fair linguist: she speaks German and French, and she brushed up her Italian, which she had learned in Florence as a girl in her teens, when the Italian sovereigns visited London. Unlike England's former Prince Consort, its present Queen speaks English without a German accent. There is only a slight exotic deposit in her voice, which is a fine contralto. (When she was young, she used to entertain after family dinner by singing sentimental ballads.) Her favorite reading is Georgian diaries, since she is historical-minded.

She has probably one of the best memories in the British Empire, certainly the best in the royal family, which is high praise, since royalty, unlike its subjects, is trained never to forget. If on remeeting a Slav singer after three years, King George can remember that the last time they met they had discussed Russian politics, and if the Prince of Wales can recall the name of an unimportant American he met on shipboard seven years before, the Queen can remember in Dresden a miniature she had merely read about twenty years before in Richmond Park. (As a married woman on tour in Tasmania, she recognized the face of a curate she had once seen preaching in England when she was a child.) She knows every piece, and on what shelf it stands, of her Chinese collections, which involve hundreds of objects; she remembers every chair in the formal furnishings of her castles' hundreds of rooms, and, if one gets mislaid, hunts it down. Her memory is ocular, not aural; by nature she is more interested in looking than in listening. Like most people with a remarkable memory, the Queen is invariably right, which is more attractive in a Queen than it would be in you or me.

She likes to dance. At village fetes at Sandringham she used to two-step with her boys' tutor, every year she dances with one of the gillies at Balmoral, and she will open the Jubilee's two great state balls by dancing the quadrille at Buckingham Palace. Indeed, like Queen Victoria, she adores dancing; unfortunately, the King, like the Prince Consort, Albert, does not. Where her mother-in-law, the fashionable Queen Alexandra, was never on time, being usually half an hour late or early, and where her own mother, the sociable Duchess of Teck, was invariably late by an hour at least, the Queen

The Jubilee Procession making its way down Fleet Street en route to Saint Paul's Cathedral.

is passionately punctual; as a child, she resolved, "on seeing the time and temper wasted in others by unpunctuality," to be on time for the rest of her life. She rises at eight when she is not going out in the morning, otherwise at seven-thirty; the King rises at six and likes to have her pour his second-breakfast cup of tea from a kitchen-variety brown earthen teapot he insists on. They receive the royal edition of the *Times,* specially printed for them on rag paper, which is like the edition used for filing in museums, but the Queen's favorite morning paper is the *Daily Telegraph.* She always turns first to page 8 (the woman's page) and Marianne Mayfayre's column, where she can usually read something about herself and her feminine relatives or friends.

The Queen likes a glass of sherry before lunch, and afterward a Virginia-tobacco, straw-tipped cigarette; the prince of Wales taught her to smoke, though apparently it's still unofficial. When she and the King are alone, they eat a typical English meal which the British sum up as "a nice cut off the joint, two vegs, a spot of cheese [the Queen likes her cheese], and a bit of a sweet." She doesn't mind a second helping of anything; also likes comforting meat pies, good heavy Yorkshire cooking on occasion, hard candies, chocolate cake, and strawberries out of season. After an Air Force dinner given for the King, he brought home to her all the extra-fine South African strawberries and asparagus that were left over. In the mornings around the palace the Queen whistles a good bit when alone in her apartments. After dinner at night, if they're with the family, she knits scarves, crochets woollies for charities, embroiders rather large petit-point palace chair-covers, since she cannot bear to be doing nothing and the King is a radio fan, which she is not. Lately she has taken slightly to jigsaw puzzles, and has a fine one of the Duke of Kent's wedding—hardly a test of her skill. When the King and she are out during the day, visiting institutions or whatever, and the King talks too long, even to the right people, or swears mildly before the wrong ones, she prods him inconspicuously with her famous umbrella and says domestically, "Now, George." When house guests ask about the K'ien-Lung cloisonné, the Chippendale chairs, the Dutch masters, the Wedgwood panels, or other art in the various palaces, the King says, like any husband, "Now, May, you know about this." And like any wife, she does, too. When they are in country residence in Norfolk, the most informal of their habitats, where in theory he is the local squire and she the squire's wife, she pours the afternoon tea if guests are few, and he passes it around. To every simple woman in England, the Queen stoutly Stands For The Home—though her homes are Buckingham Palace in the winter and summer seasons, Windsor castle over Easter, Sandringham House in the autumn and over Christmas, Balmoral Castle in August, and sometimes the royal yacht at Cowes. Behind the medieval British regalia and jewels, the King and Queen are an up-to-date, conscientious, hard-working, mutually dependent, domestic, bourgeois couple about whom there has never been an atom of marital scandal, who have reared a large family with the usual parental hopes and disappointments, who have ceaselessly labored for twenty-five years to serve the crowns they occasionally wear, and who are now growing old together in the full sight of the nation. The combination of public pomp and private life they represent is constitutionally monarchical, universally suffraged, twentieth-century England's royal ideal. The present Jubilee is a loyal celebration. It will also

Sandringham House.

be, everyone more democratically hopes, the biggest money-spending festival since the war. It has been privately affirmed and would be officially denied that the Silver Jubilee was the Queen's idea. Certainly it wasn't English history's, which normally fetes only golden anniversaries, and it wasn't the King's, an ill man, tired of parades. The Queen has the most sagacious, courageous Big Business head in the family.

According to British industrialists, she and the Prince of Wales are rated as the two best commercial salesmen in the Empire. This is unfair. The Queen is the two best salesmen. The Prince by what he wears and buys, is a special style-setter. No matter what the Queen wears, what she buys, whether stylish or not, it goes the general rounds of the Dominions. "The Queen's shopping," remarks a semi-official paper, "is one of Her Majesty's services to the Empire." She is the most sensitive single instrument affecting British commerce today. During the depression, her shrewd insistence on maintaining the dressiness of the Courts, her arranging for extra official functions (as in 1931, when things were at their worst), her ceaselessly using her position as royal social leader able to command gaieties, or anyhow their trappings, have been a life-and-death matter to London's luxury-trades people. Her attendance at industry fairs and home-furnishing expositions, her 25 purchases of an electric icebox for Buckingham Palace and labor-saving devices and modern sanitation for other royal residences, are of paramount importance to manufacturers. Her shopping expeditions collect throngs in the streets involved. She personally buys three Buckingham Palace roomfuls of Christmas presents annually, from three-shilling-sixpence remembrances for everyone on her estates, through more personal gifts for her favorite saleswomen, on up to jewels, jades, bibelots, or silver-and-enamel fitted dressing cases for her family and friends. And the year round she sends wedding presents of gems, crystal, and gold and a steady stream of smaller gifts in return for the presents she receives daily. This spring, at the age of sixty-eight, she walked seven miles among the stands on the opening day of the British Industries Fair, spent over a hundred pounds, principally on ladies' handbags, which she can never resist, ordered Australian quince and peach jams for the palace, investigated Deeside bilberries, Dundee herrings; bought paintboxes for the royal grandchildren, brooches made of bread to resemble flowers and a copy of an 1887 jubilee umbrella; discussed scone-making at an Irish bakery booth, ordered her next year's Christmas cards while she was about it, was repeatedly photographed, and finished fresh as a daisy, having

"No matter where she might be, no one could mistake her for anyone but the Queen of England."

The Prince of Wales receiving his mother, Her Majesty the Queen.

arrived a bit before ten—considerably before she was expected—and not
having stopped till one-thirty. It evidently was not enough, since she went
back on two other days for more. On these Fair treks, the Queen wears down
her young daughters-in-law and wears out the officials and press at her heels.
The handbags she bought at Olympia (she was really looking for bathmats)
were at once marked "Purchased by Her Majesty the Queen," and ordered
by every jobber and merchant from Toronto to Cape Town. She also bought
what the papers called "a new design of woollen underclothing" for the
King; whatever it was, other British husbands were soon buttoned into it.
When she bought his famous brown teapots at Marks & Spencer, a cheap
bazaar—the Queen enjoys a bargain—the pot stock was immediately ex-
hausted by humble housewives longing to buy like their Queen and for once
being able to afford it. A manufacturer of a novelty called cotton taffeta
figured that her patronage jumped his initial sales 300 per cent. They may

afterward have dropped to below zero. Even the Queen of England can't make miracles stick in a world real with unemployment.

By act of Parliament she and the King receive a hundred and ten thousand pounds annually as their combined Privy Purse, but in 1931 the King announced a voluntary cut of fifty thousand pounds, which has been in effect for the last four years. In addition, there are grants for the salaries and expenses of the royal household, which, with other appropriations, bring the royal "Civil List" to a total of four hundred and twenty thousand pounds, not counting the annuities paid to other members of the family. Being of the old economic school which believes in buying its way out of the depression, the Queen spends her share of the Privy Purse Buying British, a scheme she thought of long before the slogan was necessary or invented. In her trousseau forty-two years ago, she stipulated that every thread of silk, cambric, and wool must come from British looms only. If she is Britain's best salesman, she is also its most conscientious consumer.

Certainly she is also its most heroic hostess. Besides the ten thousand men and women annually invited to the Royal Garden Party, about eight thousand women are presented each year at the four Courts held in Buckingham Palace; four thousand invitations will also be sent out to this year's state balls. Added to these twenty-two thousand guests will be those of the state banquets—diplomats, ministers, dominion representatives. For the balls, the great scarlet-and-white ballroom will be thrown open with Yeomen of the Guard lining the staircase; in the supper room, the famous royal gold plate will be on view, as will the Queen herself, on state occasions a superb sight. For the Queen quite simply looks her best with a diamond crown on her head, wearing décolletage, loaded with royal jewels, and seated on a throne. No longer young and never a beauty, she puts beautiful young women around her in the shade. She has the classic handsome back, the impressive stately bosoms for roped pearls, the tractable curled coiffure of another generation, and the fine old-fashioned skin that companioned them. Above all she has, strengthened by etiquette and softened by her profound personal belief, the grand queenly manner of which she is the last living great example. Her trained Court gowns are of the richest pale fabrics, shot with silver or gold; are elaborate in cut; in detail beaded, embroidered, gusseted, gored, looped, draped, cap-sleeved; have no connection with any other style being practiced on earth, and are perfect. Her jewels are the finest royal European collection now remaining. She possesses three historical crowns— the seventeenth-century crown of Queen Mary of Modena (James II's consort), studded with magnificent diamonds and pearls, and rare in being devoid of colored stones; she has the same lady's coronet, also of diamonds and pearls of unusual size; and, finest of all, the Queen has her own state coronation crown, containing two of the Star of Africa diamonds, weighing 96 and 64 carats respectively, and the Koh-i-Noor, or Mountain of Light, the most famous diamond in the world, by bad cutting reduced from 800 to its present 106 carats. Her pearls are some of the finest known, including a rope that Mary, Queen of Scots, brought from France, and which on her death Queen Elizabeth paid three thousand pounds for. James I gave them

"For the Queen quite simply looks her best with a diamond crown on her head, wearing décolletage, loaded with royal jewels, and seated on a throne."

The Duchess of Kent.

The Royal Family at Ascot.

to his daughter when she married the Elector Palatine of the Rhine; they returned to England with George I, and under Queen Victoria were declared by the House of Lords to be "vested as heirlooms forever in the British crown." There are also pearls given by Drake to Queen Elizabeth. From Queen Mary's Hungarian grandmother, she has two pearl earstuds of such size that one of her ancestors cut one open with his sword to see if it was real; it was, and it had to be put together again. Her Teck pearls the Queen presented to Princess Marina. In one of the Queen's pearl parures, the necklace's outer rope, which falls to her waist, contains about a hundred and fifty enormous pearls; there are three shorter inner strands, the dog collar is nine strands high, and the crown matches. With the notable exception of some favorite old-fashioned jewelry Queen Victoria gave her, the Queen has recently had many of her stones reset and modernized. At Courts, she usually wears her gems in alternating "sets"—diamonds with pearls or emeralds or sapphires. The last, since she loves pale blue as a color even for tweeds, are obviously her favorite stones. Her sables are those given her by the late Czar.

Something must also be said about the Queen's street clothes—that she's probably been right about them after all. As a young duchess-bride, and later as the Princess of Wales, she tried to follow the big-picture-hat styles of the gay Edwardians, but it wasn't in her. It was not until, as a Queen, she discovered toques, worn high on the head like a crown—and today, in her case, practically ranking as one—that she got into her singular sartorial stride. It was lengthened by her hating black and loving light colors, aided by her insistence on being comfortable, and abetted by nobody's daring to argue with her. For twenty-five years it has been the Queen's story that she dresses in the height of fashion, which is now nearly true—for queens. In those years she has resisted hints from dressmakers, worn her skirts long when skirts were rising, raised hers, slightly, when it was too late; her hats, during her sons' sensitive sartorial twenties, caused them pain. Today she satisfies everyone, even her family. She looks like herself, with the elegant eccentricities—the umbrella or cane, the hydrangea-colored town suits, the light lizard slippers, the tip-tilted toque—of a wealthy white-haired *grande dame* who has grown into the mature style she set for herself too young.

Gowns for the Queen to choose from are brought by saleswomen to the palace after breakfast. There are no mannequins to confuse the issue—Her Majesty just holds a dress up against herself and looks in the mirror to get the general effect. The King has a big word to say. On the whole he likes ladies' clothes as they were and is on the conservative side; both of them are what dressmakers call "anti-fashion" in their taste. There's probably not a lot of direct profit in dressing the Queen. She pays only about twenty guineas for her day dresses and twenty-five for her fifteen annual evening gowns, a bit more if they are Court affairs. And she takes considerable expensive yardage. But where the Queen buys with old-fashioned economy, newfangled ladies will flock to give a fancier price. In England, royalty pays. In winter the Queen wears pale-as-she-dares long coats and dresses; in summer paler suits; never sweaters at any season. All her life she has bought most of her clothes from the two rival houses of Reville, but now orders also at Handley-Seymour's. The Queen makes up with old-fashioned delicacy— powder on her cheeks and a soupçon of rouge, her lips reddened faintly; all

The Royal Garden Party, one of the most important social events of the London season, held on the Buckingham Palace grounds.

this is officially denied but remains pleasantly visible on Her Majesty's face. Her maids are called her dressers; there are two or three, under a head dresser. In getting herself fundamentally ready for the day, the Queen is Spartan; to the dresser who laces her stays she says no word but "Pull." Nothing much is ever thrown away out of her closets; her old clothes are bagged and tagged, are remade a lot or passed on to her poorer royal relatives. She gave a flowered peignoir to a grandniece who turned up in it, remade as a dress, at the Royal Garden Party. The Queen and she were delighted.

On the word of her authorized biographer, outside of being the Queen of England, her life has been unsensational.

As a child, she has said, she was "very happy and very uninteresting." She was born on the stroke of midnight on May 26, 1867, in Kensington Palace, in the same room Queen Victoria had been born in. The future Queen's father, the Duke of Teck, immediately noted in his diary that she had "fine powerful lungs;" she was named Victoria Mary Augusta Louise Olga Pauline Claudine Agnes, but her mother called her "May" or sometimes "my Mayflower." A year or so later her mother wrote that the baby had "a most perfect figure, is wonderfully forward for her age in all things save one, her teeth, at present possessing only two bottom ones." Three brothers, the Princes Adolphus, Francis, and Alexander, soon followed. The Duchess of Teck had made an impecunious love match; her husband had first set foot on England on March 6, 1866, and by April 6 they were engaged. The Duchess, born in Hanover, was the youngest daughter of the Duke of Cambridge, who had married Princess Augusta, the youngest daughter of the Landgrave Frederick of Hesse and of Princess Caroline of Nassau-Usingen. The Queen's father, born in Vienna, was the Duke of Teck, the first Count Hohenstein, only son

33

of Duke Alexander of Württemberg and the beautiful Hungarian Claudine, Comtesse de Rhédey, who had been trampled to death by cavalry when thrown from her horse at military maneuvers. The present Queen of England is, then, in other words—and the easiest for Americans to understand— the great-granddaughter of our last King, George III. Her mother was, thus, Queen Victoria's cousin, but accounted as not very considerable royalty. In state processions she had to ride with her back to the horses, and was delighted when the populace discovered her there, which it always did, with cheers, she being, whether considerable or not, the most popular female royalty of the reign. She frankly loved being royal, and the cheers from the populace. She was portly and corseted to an hour-glass shape, usually wore terrific brocades, animated her mornings with dressing her hair and reading the novels of her friend Mr. Disraeli, called her children "the precious chicks," loved to listen to nightingales, was kindness incarnate, gave away more than she possessed, and had a dashing talent for happy life, rare in the family and time. The Duke disapproved of sports for young females, found it repugnant to see his little daughter May "even in the garden" without gloves, and seems to have been a stickler. The little daughter was presented by a Kensington butcher with a goat and cart, which, since it was raining, she first drove in the palace corridor. She saw her first elephant at the Holborn Amphitheatre and was duly impressed, for she was always sensible about relative values. She had three grades of petticoats—cotton for every day, linen for second, and embroidery for Sunday best—and early knew the great difference. When the child was half-grown, Queen Victoria moved the Tecks from Kensington Palace to White Lodge, Richmond Park. The gatekeeper said that Princess May was then a "tall, thin little girl in a short frock, white socks, high-topped boots . . . she grew up to be very genteel and ladylike." The growing-up at White Lodge continued until she left it as a bride, except when she was sixteen and the Tecks, unusually unable to make two ends meet, spent eighteen months trying to economize in Florence while she learned about Italian art. At nineteen, Princess May simultaneously made her London debut and the discovery, so she said, that she "was not educated;" for the next seven years, until her marriage, she read six hours daily with her governess, Madame Bricka, a tactless Alsatian with radical, good brains, who was one of the two major mental influences then forming the Queen of today. The reading was stiff for a debutante: the nineteenth-century European historians and philosophers then the mode, plus Carlyle, George Eliot, and the strange Rossettis. The other influence was "Gussy," as the Duchess of Teck called her elder sister—the Princess Augusta Caroline, Grand Duchess of Mecklenburg-Strelitz, a sturdy-headed old lady who grasped politics and wasn't afraid of opinions about important things then in the air. In the air were Darwin, Swinburne, Pre-Raphaelitism, the socialism of William Morris, the Select Committees' lordly inquiry into sweatshops, and—more faintly and shrilly—something which sounded like Votes for Women, though nobody could believe his ears. Together the young Princess and the elderly Duchess listened to the various new sounds.

The interruption of this life came at twenty-four, when Princess May's betrothal to the Duke of Clarence, eldest son of the Prince of Wales and heir presumptive to the British throne, was announced. Two months later, and five weeks before the date set for their marriage, he was dead of influenza.

A year and a half later, on July 6, 1893, she was married to his younger brother, the Duke of York and the new heir presumptive. The *Morning Post* said, "The marriage of one who is ultimate heir to the throne is not an event which can be regarded as purely of a private character." The *Times* said, "There is even ground for hoping that a union rooted in painful memories may prove happy beyond the common lot." The public was given a choice of two romantic legends about the bride: one that she had really loved the elder brother, the other that actually she had always been in love with the younger brother. Twenty-six years before, the morning after the Princess was born, chroniclers had pointed out that she was cousin to the two royal princes—but not too near a cousin. Whether they were later her choices, or she was theirs, it is known that she was Queen Victoria's. The bride spent her honeymoon at York Cottage, an overflow Sandringham guest house that Edward built in his princely days; five of her six children were subsequently born there. In the nursery are still visible the mottoes which the little Princes, David, Bertie, Harry, Georgie, embroidered—pious phrases such as "Dear Mamma," "Feed My Lambs," and "Look Unto Jesus." The daughter, Princess Mary, seemed fonder of making windmills.

It was a seventeen years' apprenticeship before the Queen reached the throne. They were not happy public years for her, especially those nine she spent (after Queen Victoria's death in 1901) as Princess of Wales. She had turned thirty-four to begin her task, was already settled in her serious-minded, shy mold, was a dowdy royal dresser with nothing, even when she was

Royal brothers: the Duke of Kent, the Prince of Wales, the
Duke of York, and the Duke of Gloucester.

later crowned Queen, but her fine, fair hair to compete in public popularity against the gay, stylish beauties who had made up the long Edwardian rout—Mrs. Lillie Langtry, Lady de Grey, Lady Londonderry, and at their head her hopelessly handsome, enameled mother-in-law, the powerful Dowager Queen Alexandra. Indubitably another snobbish wrong militating against her popularity had also been done the Queen, even when betrothed: much had been made of her being "such an English princess," but too much had been made of her being "not a considerable royal personage" by birth, compared with her spouse. At their coronation (which the Socialist party gloomily called an anachronism anyhow), the Archbishop introduced a special phrase to cover her case, praying that "by the powerful and mild influence of her piety and virtue she may adorn the dignity which she hath obtained." Yet from her Cambridge mother's side, such mutual blood flowed in the Queen's and King's veins as to make them second cousins once removed. As for the unfair rating given her paternal ancestry, she tried to repair it by laboriously compiling the Teck genealogy and presenting a copy to the Heralds' College, but little notice seems to have been taken of it.

The Queen as an individual was not really popular until the war. In those blasting four years, foreign nepotisms and local snobberies were destroyed, and the Queen, by her unexpected administrative brilliance in women's war work, by her sensitiveness to the new problems of feminine labor and feminism, by her sense for organization and her impatience with red tape, by her long hospital service and her tireless energy, began to become the admired and beloved popular public personage she is in England today. Her Majesty's vast Central Committee had for four years virtual charge of all paid female labor in England. It effected the transfer of millions of women from peace to war industries, and, according to the Queen's only authorized biographer, Kathleen Woodward, saved the government from threatened industrial troubles. Margaret Bondfield, the first British woman Minister of Labor, said that it had also "saved the self-respect of countless women workers." The late, powerful Mary Macarthur of the National Federation of Women Workers, who eventually was to become a real friend of the Queen, cooperated with the committee from its inception. The committee finally took over from the Royal Army clothing department the job of making shirts for the entire British Army. The Queen's Needlework Guild was the patriotic outlet for the upper-class unpaid women workers, and served to send 15.5 million articles to 744 regiments; her Collecting Fund brought in one thousand pounds daily. Often the Queen spent three or four hours a day in the military hospitals, visiting especially the facial wards the lesser visitors couldn't stomach. With only a lady-in-waiting, she spent ten days in France, talked to every living Englishman in every English base hospital she visited, and officially cheered up the VADs, the WAACs, and her other feminine organizations. In none of these administrative activities did the Queen sit on the sidelines; she was in the center, asking questions, getting answers, working like a nailer; and, helping England, she was in her element. In unloosing her energies during those four years, her character stepped forth free. Her hair turned white during the war.

However, her peacetime occupations have been nearly as energetic. In her official lifetime she has completely rearranged the furnishing of the royal residences in England and Holyrood Palace and Balmoral Castle in

Scotland. (King Edward originally started the work, but at Windsor only.) The job has consisted of separating and styling, in thousands of palace rooms, the millions of chairs, pictures, tables, chromos, china shepherdesses, fringed sofas, and whatnots of every domestic and foreign period from early Bourbon down to late Gladstone, which time and especially Queen Victoria had allowed to mix into a permanent sentimental muddle. The English consider the Queen pretty much of an expert on house arrangements, tasteful placing of objects, and the like. Certainly she is an expert on things Middle Georgian, being authoritative on the diaries, furniture, and china of the period, all of which she collects copiously. About such things, she not only knows, she cares, which makes her good. About antiques in general she's acquisitive. Her great, individual, rich collection is, however, her Chinese objects, some being examples of really remarkable quality. Her jades are principally eighteenth-century—she isn't interested in the earlier tomb or ritual jades—and she's very fond of the jeweled jades made up for the Indian Mogul market. A few specially fine Chinese items among her many splendid hundreds are a superb seventeenth-century spice box of ruby-studded white mutton fat (a color of jade she likes only next best to green), two lavender-colored jade rice bowls penciled with gold—a very rare type of K'ien-Lung work—and some red Fuchow lacquer. She has cabinets full of exquisite miniature jade pieces and little objects in other hard stones. Her Canton enamels, notably the miniature tea sets, the vases, and cloisonné ducks and elephants, are exceptional. She has been collecting jades for at least thirty years and was one of the first to do so in a large way, since the stones began to come out freely from China only after the Boxer campaign. Most of her finer pieces come from the famous London antiquarian J. Sparks, who considers Her Majesty "very knowledgeable." She has installed a Chinese room at Buckingham Palace, where there are Buddhas, some of them with heads that nod. As the Queen walks through, she taps them with her finger and they sit assenting as she passes by.

Her other eccentric hobby is her famous doll's house; she has a passion for what the English call Tinycraft, meaning anything little which should be big. The doll's house, which is kept at Windsor, was designed by the great architect Sir Edwin Lutyens, to show posterity what a 1923 rich British home was like. It is scaled one inch to one foot, and is one hundred inches long and sixty-two inches wide. The outer walls lift off, revealing within crazily complete, elegant furnishings, all practicable, all in scale, including a wine cellar, fishing rods, a library of postage-stamp-sized books handwritten by Milne, Maugham, Conan Doyle, et al., an insurance policy, toilets, baths, towels, and water that runs. Two tomes on the doll's house have been compiled wherein the cellar is nobly described by Professor George Saintsbury, the nurseries by Lady Cynthia Asquith. The doll's house has to be seen to be believed.

The Queen does not waste her administrative ability on the household details of the various larger royal dwellings as long as they go right. When they go wrong, she becomes executive. Skeleton staffs of servants are maintained in the non-London houses, with part of the Buckingham Palace staff sensibly sent on to fill in when the King and Queen are coming; linen, too, is sent on from the Buckingham Palace supply (as large as a hotel's), traveling back and forth under the eye of Mrs. Moore, the housekeeper. Some of the coarser royal napery is made of the flax from the King's new fields on his Norfolk estate; the Queen is interested in experiments in hand-dyeing the linen, though she herself really likes only white on a table. In journeying to Sandringham or on state affairs, the Queen travels in one of her electrically footwarmed automobiles—a private green limousine, and an official car in the royal colors of purple and scarlet. The preferred make of the elder members of the family is the Daimler. What is called the Queen's Household consists at present of sixteen ladies of high degree chosen from among the Queen's intimate friends. Their duties are mostly nominal and amiable, though in olden days they were literal. For twenty-five years, the Queen's Mistress of the Robes, the highest in position, has been the Duchess of Devonshire; at the opening of Parliament and when the Queen holds Court, the Mistress of the Robes must be present. A royal coach is sent to fetch her on the former occasion; on the latter, when decorations are being worn, she wears her unique badge of office, a miniature of the Queen set in brilliants. There are four regular Ladies of the Bedchamber, three Extra Ladies of the Bedchamber, six Women of the Bedchamber, one Extra Woman of the Bedchamber, one Maid of Honor. Only four, the Queen's favorites, are in regular attendance: two Ladies of the Bedchamber, Baroness Ampthill, who comes to Buckingham Palace by bus, and Mabell, Countess of Airlie; and two Women of the Bedchamber, Lady Bertha Dawkins and Lady Cynthia Colville. All the Household interest themselves in the Queen's charities, of which the three principal ones are the Girls' Friendly Society, the London Needlework Guild, and the Personal Service League. Each year, when the day comes for classifying the garments sent in for distribution among the poor, the Queen wears an apron at the task; annually the apron gets in the newspapers. She sensibly believes in letting the rich climbers of all faiths who might become ample subscribers to her causes get a glimpse of the inside of the palace at select, aristocratic charity meetings. Like most women who are helpless to combat it, the Queen has an enormous conscience about poverty, especially about the housing conditions of the poor. She's seen the slums of London; her astringent comments on such official trips have helped clean up certain of the worst East End districts. On such visits she puts on her most hydrangea-tinted, queenly clothes, wearing what those who want to see her want her to wear. She's a downright favorite with the poor; they like to stare at her and exclaim, "Ain't she a fair bloomin' treat!" Among the slum districts she has worked enormously for the establishment of infant welfare and maternity centers and hospitals. It would be officially denied, but the best private authorities state, and with admiration for her courage, that the Queen is behind the birth-control movement recently permitted increasing propaganda in England.

Her Majesty's correspondence is vast and varied. Letters come, addressing her as anything from Mrs. Queen to Madame Majesty, and advise her to rub camphorated oil on her husband's chest, because it did the writer's husband's chest good; or hope that the Prince of Wales has a nice birthday, because he was born on the writer's wedding morn, so she'll never forget him; or maybe ask the Queen why she was out having a good time at the races at Ascot (which she probably wasn't, as she dislikes sport) when there's so much unemployment. The Queen opens her mail herself; on the back of each envelope she scribbles the answer, which her secretaries send, type-written, unstamped, and franked "Privy Purse." In the ordinary course of events, a letter received at Buckingham Palace on one day is answered by the next, for the Queen is *démodée* enough to think that promptness is still a part of good manners. On the rare occasions when she answers communications herself, her letters are in her longhand and, often enough, not signed with the official "Mary R." Her writing is slanting, angular, with high pointed staffs and a longish swing between the small letters—an oddly poetic script for such a busy, practical ruler.

Her worldly position is curious. Verbally she is addressed as "Ma'am" by all subjects who are gentlefolk or above, and by all below as "Your Majesty." Legally she is rather like what old English law calls a *feme sole*, ordinary wives being *feme covert*, since from early times an English King's Consort has had the right of transacting her own affairs, just as if she weren't married. The Queen can't be fined in any court, or be made to pay a toll, yet she can sue and be sued in her own name with the affix "Queen of England." "To compass or imagine her death [during the lifetime of her husband] is high treason." She is traditionally entitled to the tail of any whale taken on English coasts, to use in the boning of her corsets.

The Queen is now in her best years. At the age of fifty she began, mistakenly, to fear the advance of time. Since then her children have matured, bringing the increased mutual satisfaction and sympathy usual in adult relationships between the generations. Like most earnest mothers, she has sometimes been given pain or worry by her sons, one way or another. The Prince of Wales and the Duke of Kent have been the most modernizing, modifying filial influences; there's a story one yearns to believe that the Prince once took his mother riding on a roller coaster. The most softening of her family attachments has indubitably been that which she feels for her little granddaughter the Princess Elizabeth, at the moment presumptive future Queen of England in her own right. Just as Queen Mary looks exactly like her great-grandmother Queen Charlotte, so Princess Elizabeth looks exactly like her grandmother Queen Mary. Or as cockney curb admirers say on seeing the two driving out together, "She's the spit of her granny." If she overhears it, the Queen invariably beams.

Queen Mary's life has been one of inhuman self-control. The earthly honors have been heavy; the present Silver Jubilee, loaded though it is with pomp and presence, must at least seem light with satisfaction for the quarter century now safely past. On the state drives through London the Queen will look wonderful, bowing from inside her royal landau. No matter where she might be, no one could mistake her for anyone but the Queen of England.

Edith Evans and Ruth Gordon [*opposite*] in *The Country Wife*.

1936

Lᴏɴᴅᴏɴ's hotels, snack bars, theatres, cinemas, tubes, buses, flatlets, lodging houses, art shows, antique dealers' shops, bridle paths, and sidewalks are full. London is now unlike any London seen since the war. London's passion for going to the play has particularly profited. *The Country Wife*, which authorities declare to be the coarsest of Wycherley's Restoration comedies, has for this reason, along with others, been the town's most uproariously popular piece ever since its recent revival at the Old Vic. Apparently Wycherley suits us as he suited no other age but his own. After a Drury Lane production in 1748, the play was discreetly ignored until the Phoenix Society put it on in 1924. Since then it has been three times revived. In its latest recrudescence, the debut of Ruth Gordon as the country wife was of extreme interest to enthusiastic critics who not only forgave her for talking American but even accepted the Broadway accent as a further proof of rusticity. Certainly Miss Gordon gives a remarkable, if varied, performance. She speaks Mr. Wycherley's lines as if they had been written by Dorothy Parker; in her manner, there is more of *Seventeen* than of the seventeenth century. However, beneath her mugging, there are self-knowledge, experience, timing, and a willful reinterpretation often incomprehensible to the English audience, but which is appreciated by it with shouts of mirth when Miss Gordon rises to the jerky peaks of the pure comic, as in

40

her nightgown struggles and her heroic footlight grunt during the famous letter-writing scene. In contrast to her Mistress Pinchwife is the Lady Fidget of London's Edith Evans, a creation without a tremble, without a blush, a smooth mixture of lovely voice and lively vice, a perfect portrait such as could be found parading only on England's stage.

Next month, the BBC starts its first afternoon and evening television programs, to be presented daily except Sunday. This new service, and the preliminary tests at Alexandra Palace, are, of course, mere practice periods

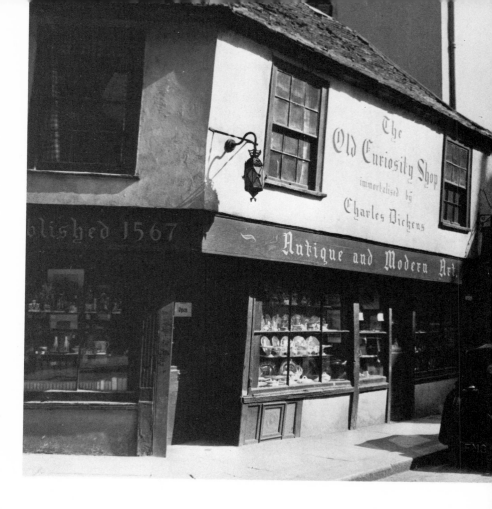

leading up to next year's ambitious attempt to televise the Coronation of Edward VIII.* To date, televisionary results are more interesting than satisfactory. Twenty-five miles is about as far as the pictures carry without blurring; the frames are too small to contain a crowd, and the Coronation scenes will principally be composed of crowds; the electrical apparatus belonging to doctors on Harley Street, though nowhere near Alexandra Palace, has interfered with transmission; and at one time a performer tearing some paper too close to the camera almost ruined that day's performance. The promised rooms in which the public may view television are still scarce. At present, television can be seen chiefly at Selfridge's department store, the South Kensington Science Museum, and Waterloo Station. Also, the high cost of commercial receiving sets has been no help, though *Television*, the new fan magazine here, has published instructions on how to build a cheap makeshift set at home.

In London, as in New York, music accompanies money. As the most prosperous capital in Europe, London will doubtless be the most musical one this winter. The melodic season began principally with Sir Thomas Beecham's shifting his famous Sunday-afternoon concerts from Queen's Hall to Covent

42   * King George V had died on January 20, 1936.

Garden, and with the demonstration, despite his detractors, of the indubitable improvement he has forced on the London Philharmonic in the last few years. Its violins are still too sweet, but its bold brasses have been tempered. In the Philharmonic's recent performance of Berlioz's *Symphonie Fantastique*, there was an effect of genius which stiffened the listeners with excitement and reduced Sir Thomas's pompous collar to a rag. The real fault in London's symphonic efforts lies not in the scarcity of orchestras, of which London, reputed to be unmusical, has four, but in the public's too ample and conservative appetite for symphonic pieces. The BBC Orchestra, which has grown to be one of the best, has just announced that, as usual, it will run through the classic symphonies in the course of the season; that it will discontinue the winter Proms, and that it loses money on all public appearances —to which Toscanini's scheduled six spring appearances should be a rich exception. Because London listeners are what they themselves call conservative, all these bands must repeatedly feature the classic symphonies, which are not sufficient to supply variety in the current overproduction of music on the air and in the halls. It's the limited supply of truly great music which has recently popularized Sibelius in London, which finally aided Delius, which revived Chabrier in France, and, if the Vienna Symphony is lucky in its approaching rendering here of Bruckner's Seventh, may add Bruckner and even Mahler to the London lists. The *Times* says it looks forward with excitement to the season's presentation of Bax's Sixth and Hindemith's *Mathis der Maler*, though it adds that it had hoped for the latter's *Cardillac* or Berg's *Wozzeck*. In London, the times have certainly changed.

"London is a great metropolis, crowded with people, all of them living courteously crammed together." Regent Street shoppers.

A small but perfect exhibition of "Masters of Nineteenth-Century French Painting" has opened at the New Burlington Galleries under the auspices of the Anglo-French Art and Travel Society, which is composed of hundreds of backers from among the noblest families in the Kingdom. Lord Ivor Churchill compiled the catalogue; few of the canvases have ever been publicly shown in England before. Perhaps the newest thing about the exhibition is Anthony Blunt's curious article explaining the canvases' styles in the light of the painters' politics—with Daumier's proletarian paintings seen as a reaction to the failure of the Commune; Monet driven, like all the bourgeoisie, from realism into abstraction; Manet representing the new *nouveaux riches*; Corot free to paint his best because his class, shopkeepers, had won their liberty, and he could afford to leave town during the Revolution of 1830; and Gauguin seen as a defeatist produced by the industrial instability of the last years of the century. Politics are now visible everywhere in Europe. Even in oils and aquarelles.

OCTOBER 29

THE greatest Motor Show London has seen since the exhibitions were 44 started, in 1905, has been held at Olympia. Beneath a dignified red, white, and blue ceiling, what looked more like a bazaar than an exposition was attended from the moment it opened by record crowds, and purchases soon passed the £50,000,000 mark. Would-be buyers stood in queues to meet the salesmen; the Duke of Kent, who bought a Bentley which was on display, had his hat knocked off in the crush; orders came in over long-distance telephone from Africa and Australia; and it was announced that the distributors had sent in exceptionally heavy orders for the Morris, which is England's Ford. Indeed, the Morris created a stir on the Stock Exchange and at healing centers as well as at the Motor Show, for Lord Nuffield, the former Mr. Morris, caused excitement in the City by putting his common stock on the market and agitated Oxford University by presenting it with £1,350,000 *— the greatest single gift ever made here by a man during his lifetime for a public purpose—to found a medical-research school for medicine, surgery, gynecology, obstetrics, and anesthetics.

To one who, like ourself, considers the elderly, high-busted, short-chassised, speed-limited London taxi the ideal motor vehicle for comfort and dignity, the Motor Show was a bitter disappointment, being filled with thirty-two British, fourteen American, seven French, six German, and two Italian makes of cars which were magnificently long, low, and modern, and guaranteed to go too fast. Two facts about British cars stand out before the American eye. First, because of the London passion for weekending in the country, having enough luggage cupboards is considered as essential as having enough wheels. Second, there are more inexpensive British cars than formerly. In the Show's eleven price categories, which range from £118, for the Austin Seven, up to £2535, for the hauntingly beautiful Phantom III Rolls-Royce,

* The pound was approximately five dollars.

". . . the hauntingly beautiful Phantom III Rolls-Royce. . . ."

four British makes are offered in Category 1 at less than £150. What the British eye notices about British cars, is, on the contrary, that decreased taxation on horsepower and increased prosperity make higher-priced and powered motors possessable at last. The so-called 1½-litre type is today's favorite. Connected with the Motor Show was a sideshow of caravans, as superciliously superior to American trailers in installation as in name. One, which costs £320, is a four-bed affair with pink silk puffs and every luxury, including a vase of flowers in the back window. Ford's perennially separate exhibit, at the Albert Hall, was less a sideshow than vaudeville. It was advertised as "Twelve Hours Without a Dull or Boring Moment," and featured a V-8 Shadow-Symphony Orchestra, radio music, movies, the dismantling and reassembling of an engine in fifteen minutes, a demonstration class from the Ford trade school, and a magic trick in which the body of a Ford V-8 disappeared right under your nose. European motor manufacturers wouldn't mind if all Fords disappeared.

With London offering the most vital atmosphere of any capital in Europe as an inducement to keep them at home, Londoners are traveling about the world in the biggest voyage boom known since Clive of India. Thomas Cook is offering an irresistible junket entitled "Across Africa in the Steps of Livingstone," which, though it doesn't include Stanley, promises everything else—the Benguela Railway, Lobito, Angola, the Belgian Congo, Rhodesia, and the Johannesburg Exhibition. Next in thrills is the Booth Line's "One Thousand Miles Up the Amazon," with organized excursions ashore, and Portugal, Madeira, and Brazil as side bait. The *Bremen* and the *Europa* are offering excursion rates to what many Britons still rank as the wilds—Florida, Niagara Falls, Detroit, Washington. The new and much-needed London-to-Paris sleeping cars are booked solid for the next fortnight because Europe's monetary alignment has resulted in bargain offers, which are advertised with candor: "Italy Is Still the Cheapest—99 Lire to the £—Winter Sports with Sunshine Guaranteed," "Outwit Winter with the Devaluated Franc," "Visit the Swiss Riviera, Where the £ Is Now Worth 40% More."

However, the one spot about which the English are worrying, for fear they won't get to it, is a window overlooking the Coronation procession. Owners of space along the line of march are asking such exorbitant prices that single window seats are quoted at thirty guineas by reputable agencies which beg their clients not to buy. The agents have declared the situation a racket, since a price of ten guineas should suffice for a spectacle that will last less than five minutes, and have furthermore lodged their protest with Earl Stanhope, First Commissioner of Works, whose office has charge of seating facilities. The vast public to which a price of ten guineas is as wild as one of thirty is pinning its hopes not on an Earl but on its King. The people feel he is so democratic he will insist on there being some cheap seats so that England's democracy can see him the day he is crowned. Certainly his ideas about money values are definite. To avoid the heavy loss at which his fifteen-thousand-acre estate at Sandringham has always been run, he is reducing his staff of workers from seven hundred to three hundred. Those dismissed are to

King Edward VIII inspecting the Yeomen of the Guard at the Tower of London.

receive bonuses and new jobs, some at the Royal Family's flax factory. He probably will retain only three hundred acres, which experts tell him can show a profit in two years if split up into self-supporting units and rented out. He also is dispersing his father's shire-horse stud at Anmer Farm. Twenty of the horses have just been sold at the Peterborough market. With unemployment, even of horses, still one of England's problems, it is significant that the Leftist *Herald* made no criticism of the King's Sandringham order—unless it was contained in the observation that when he inspected the estate he wore a green Tyrolean cape and hat.

The British reaction to Mrs. Simpson's divorce, in case your tabloid hasn't told you all you want to know about *that*, continues to be violently British.

NOVEMBER 4

OF all the Americans dwelling in London, Mrs. Wallis Simpson of Baltimore is most discussed by Americans. Owing to the silence of English newspapers, there are millions of English people who never discuss her because they have never heard of her. For the first five of the seven years she has lived in London, no one ever heard of her except her friends, most of whom had known her for years and were compatriots. During the past two years, she has become a London hostess of such importance that her invitations, which are given to few, have come to rank as commands. She's a remarkable hostess because she likes sociability and dislikes social obligations, because she prefers the parlor to the night club, because she never asks personal questions, and because she has a real gastronome's gift for knowing about good food. Outside of that, she's not an extraordinary American. The food she serves is probably the second major reason for her fame in a limited London circle; it already ranks her, in a town where fine dishes make a woman noticeable, with Lady Portarlington, Lady Colefax, Mrs. Hannah Gubbay, and Mrs. Gilbert Miller. Mrs. Simpson isn't pretty in any conventional manner and doesn't think she is. Her face has the length formerly seen in nineteenth-century portraits, and she can't look her best in photographs, as she easily would have in a velvet-framed daguerreotype. Her best detail is her high, well-poised forehead, which she now fully features, having lately given up the temple curls she used to minimize it. Her head has an ample cranial structure that dominates her frail body; her figure is flawless and impersonal in the modern manner; her skin is of the smooth vellum variety that takes modern makeup well, rather than the thin, rose-petal, Southern-belle type that supported nothing but rice powder. Her hands she regrets; they are competent and strong, and have stubby fingers, so she wears no rings. Instead, she wears magnificent emerald earrings, diamond clips, and bracelets. However, her feet, which in this age of Riviera sun-bathing are well known, are beautiful, small, and elegant, with classically separated toes and rouged nails.

She gets most of her clothes at Mainbocher's; she dresses simply and with a habitual neatness which is instructive. Neither her people, the Warfields,

Mrs. Wallis Warfield Simpson.

nor either of her husbands have been rich, yet she always has looked as if a corps of maids helped her out of a bandbox. At no time in her life have her friends ever seen her with a button awry; her tidiness is something neither she nor circumstances have ever been able to control.

Though she prefers to get straight to the point if that is practical, she has unusual tact, part of which is feminine, part of which amounts to diplomacy as ambassadors understand it. Recently, at a performance of *Götterdämmerung* in Vienna (she is very fond of good music, but doesn't sing or play a note), she saw to it that her less musical host, who had quitted the box, returned to it for the final curtain, so as to assure to Mme. Flagstad especially gala applause. Mrs. Simpson never worries about her personality, so she is sure of herself. She moves and speaks with authority in a rather strident American voice, which she's never tried to Anglicize, and in a Baltimore accent. Her nerves seem to be internal, not external; she has a temper she's learned to handle, and a good working sense of justice. She can be pigheaded or determined once she gets round to it, and has the American woman's tendency to reform men in small ways. She's no social snob; she still keeps up with her old friends of all sorts, though she has too much good sense to try to mix groups. Not one of her old friends has turned into a new enemy, which is a pretty remarkable tribute; she's always had a gift for friendliness and loyalty, and stands up at the drop of a hat for those she likes. She's mentally snobbish, like many American women, in that she sensibly prefers people who will instruct her, or anyhow furnish brilliant conversation. She particularly enjoys middle-aged statesmen, since they are in a position to know and are good talkers; and she's quick on the verbal trigger herself. She's a wisecracker, has an exceptional memory, is letter-for-letter accurate in her anecdotes. Her tongue is kind. She isn't much of a reader, but she can't resist reading the American press clippings; when they arrive, it's a bad day. She feels that it would be awful if she had to live up to some of them. She has a sense of humor.

She used to play a decent game of bridge, has never been a sportswoman, is terrified of flying. She's an excellent dancer and a good-natured traveler. She has gone through the average fashionable routine of the Riviera, Tunis, etc.

At her cocktail parties in her former flat on Upper George Street, for which she hand-picked her few guests, she mixed the drinks herself, using a small, low table and several shakers. She can make anything reasonable that's asked for, and without fuss; she measures the proportions with her eye, and turns out an even glassful as accurately as any barman. She doesn't drink cocktails, preferring whisky and soda; she smokes Turkish cigarettes. In addition to being a good cook herself, she can make her own cook be a good cook. She possesses choice recipes which she gives to favored friends; her chocolate cake is considered historic. In a restaurant, she can diagnose the ingredients of a good sauce by tasting it, and if she isn't sure, is likely to ask the chef; she's definitely competent in the selection of wines. In Paris she can compose a menu a Frenchman respects. When abroad, she keeps her eye open for tasty local specialties. She returned from her last visit to France with a big basket of *fraises des bois*, which she had bought for a friend. In London, no one can see how she knows that her food is good, since she hardly tastes it; she's a small, finical, simple eater. She orders well at home or in

public, gets more out of her English servants than most Englishwomen do out of theirs, and does a lot of her own household errands herself. She will shop for what she wants at the florist or Fortnum & Mason or Harrods, who carry a certain ivory-colored candle that she favors. She's by temperament hospitable, but she's never wasted a cent in her life; she knows values. It's in her nature to like housekeeping, and she does a good job of it, the way women used to. She prefers old-fashioned things—snuffboxes, eighteenth-century etuis with portraits on them, and the like. She hates modernist décor.

She has just rented, until next August, a furnished house in Regent's Park, in one of those rows of plastered and pedimented yellow mansions which are architecturally the most undisturbed George IV remnants in London. With their dignified Nash fripperies of Regency days, these mammoth dwellings outline and face the Park's large landscape of lawns, trees, and lake, where water birds fly and congregate in the heart of London. Though credited by American news-agency photographs with occupying the entire central section of Cumberland Terrace, which is big enough to house an institution, Mrs. Simpson has leased only Number 16, which is thirty feet wide; the furnishings are said to be in no way special. If her house is like others in the group, it consists of a ground floor with dining room and back room, a first floor with an L-shaped drawing room, and second and third floors with bedrooms.

Mrs. Simpson's position in London is without precedent in history, for an American. Nor have those who historically preceded her, no matter what their nationality, been remotely like her.   51

Lady Milbanke and Mrs. Dudley Ward.

Margot Asquith (Countess of Oxford).

Lady Astor and distinctive guests at her house party at Ascot.

The Honorable Mrs. Reginald Fellowes. There was a curious reinforced quality in the values which she had inherited and for which she herself stood. Beautiful, intelligent, rich, and exceptionally popular with people on various levels; mentally the superior of most of those she was surrounded by. Her fortune came from her American mother, a Singer-sewing-machine heiress. Her father was the French Duc Decazes. As a further ramification, one of her English husband's grandfathers was also the grandfather of Winston Churchill. She divided her time between London and Paris, in both of which cities she was noted as a fascinating hostess.

The King making the rounds of the distressed areas of Wales.

Three weeks ago King Edward VIII made a voluntary visit to the distressed areas of Wales where, amidst the beginning of a public enthusiasm which soon spread over the whole land, he declared to the crowds of unemployed, "I am here to help you." The visit did not help the King with Parliament. The House had not advised the tour and disapproved of the words. The tour looked like criticism, and the words, from a constitutional monarch, sounded unconstitutional. Last Tuesday, the Bishop of Bradford in a modest diocesean conference piously wished that the King gave more positive signs of awareness of his need of Divine Grace. Using the prelate as a precedent, on Wednesday the provincial press, led by the powerful *Yorkshire Post*, gave the first voice to material rumors about the King's private life. On Thursday, the London papers broke their long, self-imposed silence in a clamor of pentup news: the King of England's desire to marry the American Mrs. Wallis Warfield Simpson was stated, and a constitutional crisis was announced. Friday brought the threat of abdication. Saturday the Cabinet ministers were commanded to stay within an hour's drive of Downing Street, and Sunday was given to the strain of waiting for what had been promised as Monday's final news. In six days the traditional elements of Church, State, and King had coalesced into what England has bitterly lived through in centuries before—a struggle between Parliament and the Crown with, as a modern paradoxical novelty, Parliament urging royalness on the King and the King fighting for the rights of a common man. Whatever the version of victory was to be, it was clear that the thoroughly aroused Parliament would win it. In England now, love for the King is a profound stream of emotion. But government by representation is a flat conviction which during the last ten generations of Kings, few of whom were loved, has increasingly spread itself over the island to keep monarchy in its special precious place.

As an obstinately romantic figure apparently bent on turning a foreign citizen with odds against her into his Queen, the King was at his best during the first twenty-four hours of the struggle, when he was viewed as being

". . . the London papers broke their long, self-imposed silence in a clamor of pentup news . . . a constitutional crisis was announced."

parentally bullied by Baldwin, his Premier. But with the King's demand for either morganatic marriage or abdication, the shock at learning that the King could love anything more than England's throne established jealous realities. The late King George, "by his complete separation of his duty as King from all personal antipathies, passions, and idiosyncrasies, and by the complete subjection of his personal views," is today regarded, after his quarter-century reign, as the master of the art of constitutional kingship. Within one year his son has shown his desire chiefly to be master of his unconventional fate. With his charm, greater than that of any ruler since the troublesome Stuarts, and his sympathy for the common people, it is possible that Edward VIII approximates the type of king for tomorrow. Most of his thoughtful subjects would prefer him to be typical of today or even yesterday. Indeed, the time element is what is basically at fault. The Duke of York, who was born second, should have been King George's first-born son.

Though the English felt that part of our press had hounded Mrs. Simpson as if she were a fox, the British reporters, once let loose, showed themselves no less full-tongued in running her to her present French earth. The first night she was pictured in the prints, one paper ran twenty-seven photographs of her. When, by His Majesty's plan, she tried to slip across the Channel, a British steamer captain gave her name, his name, and the whole show away as happily as if aiding King and country. Photos of her trunks on the *quais* with a strangely jolly French porter and her initials, W.W.S., equally falsely brightened up, were printed for two days. The Blois hotel bed she slept in and, beside it, the landlady in spectacles and with a bottle of Perrier for which she probably got paid extra, were also portrayed. A map of France was kindly printed with Mrs. Simpson's progress traced so each reader had the sense of being on her track.

However, the great and important difference between the worst American and the least refined British hounding of her lay in vocabulary. It is certain that thousands of not so straightlaced English have stiffened before America's journalistic whoopla, which undeniably aided in bringing about the most serious English governmental crisis of the past hundred years.

During the recent House of Commons meeting, attendance to hear the Premier's rare, undefinitive statements has been so full that honorable members sat listening on the steps. To lessen public tension, what are called diaries of the day are printed in which, without saying what the high persons said (which is what the public wants to know), their chronological movements, between what palace and which other high person, are listed. Thus the public in the morning learns that the night before the King interviewed the Duke of York at Buckingham Palace at eight; at nine received Baldwin for fifty minutes; at ten-twenty drove to Marlborough House to see his mother; returned to Buckingham Palace shortly before midnight; and left at one-twenty by car for Fort Belvedere, where he arrived shortly before two. Around the leading protagonists revolve and are reported the secondary

The King and Mrs. Simpson in Salzburg.

worried figures—the Keeper of the Privy Purse, Royal Dukes' private secretaries and assistant private secretaries, Anthony Eden, equerries, the King's lawyer, the King's father's doctor, State cars with muffled figures inside, State cars without any figures at all inside. Behind these move the calm Londoners. To anyone accustomed to the recent agitations of Continental towns, what is called British phlegm seems a kind of conscious public conduct which broadens the belittling phrase into discipline, good manners, tolerance, and some sort of civilized trust in government as a plan. Before Mr. Baldwin's residence in Downing Street there are, besides placards reading "God Save the King—from Mr. Baldwin," crowds of working people with signs stating "After what he did in Wales don't let the King down." In a smart West End theatre the audience sang "God Save the King." On the other hand, in a Hampstead Heath neighborhood movie, the gramophone record of the national anthem was reduced to its first three phrases and quickly switched into "Let's put out the lights and go to sleep." It is before the grilles and

The scene at Marble Arch.

Stanley Baldwin, the highly respectable head of the Conservative party whose misfortune it was as Prime Minister to be unsympathetically involved with an illicit Royal love affair. It was not in his nature to be a popular public figure.

gate of Buckingham Palace that the largest crowds find their most permanent and coldest meeting place. In raw wind and rain, night and morning, hundreds gather to wait, to look, to warm themselves occasionally with a shrill "Long Live the King!" And though the King they get to live longest with them may be the new George VI, the King they mean is Edward VIII.

DECEMBER 13

King Edward's abdication on December 11 was very much like a funeral. Popular grief was instinctively felt for someone who had gone forever, even before the government executed the formula announcing the demise of the Crown. As long as there was hope of saving a monarch who was constitutionally ailing, but adored, the people stood silently around the Houses of Parliament and Buckingham Palace as around sickbeds. When Edward gave out the news of his own legal death, they accepted the less lovable man

INSTRUMENT OF ABDICATION

I, Edward the Eighth, of Great
Britain, Ireland, and the British Dominions
beyond the Seas, King, Emperor of India, do
hereby declare My irrevocable determination
to renounce the Throne for Myself and for
My descendants, and My desire that effect
should be given to this Instrument of
Abdication immediately.

In token whereof I have hereunto set
My hand this tenth day of December, nineteen
hundred and thirty six, in the presence of
the witnesses whose signatures are subscribed.

SIGNED AT
FORT BELVEDERE
IN THE PRESENCE
OF

Edward RI

Albert

Henry.

George.

"The crisis was over."

who had been put in his place, and went to the theatre and cinema. When "God Save the King" was played at the conclusion of the performance, they rose for the one as they had risen for the other, put on their coats, and went home. The crisis was over. Passions had run high for a week, and softened only for a moment into tears when, introduced by the announcer as Prince Edward, the former King invisibly addressed the people on the air.

What the disappointed masses had said about their ex-monarch the night before his radio talk was not printed because it was unprintable. The quietest comment was "He's let us down." There were also dubious limericks. Though on the King's side the struggle had begun as one of emotions, the final battle was fought in ink. Had printing presses and cameras not been invented, the King, through word of mouth, might in the course of months have won over masses accustomed through centuries to long legends of love. Today, such stories are illustrated by flashlight photographs and, worse, told by stop-press news. Furthermore, England's most powerful pair of papers, the Sunday and the daily *Times*, were harshly anti-King and pro-Parliament. They called Edward a rebel, quoted Clarendon's three-hundred-year-old lament about "impetuous passyons," and referred editorially to infatuations.

As for the so-called King's press, Lord Rothermere's papers printed a weak defense of morganatic marriage, which, once it was legalized, they said, need never be heard of again—an odd formula for making English history. While millions of humble Britons, kindled by the rarity of a monarch's love for love, flamed at first in support of Edward's marrying, like themselves, whom he chose, as days drew on their sentiment changed, since quitting the job and engaging in a left-handed wedding were not what they'd had in mind. Nor were they consulted any more than if they had been members of Parliament. By law, the matter lay between the King and his Cabinet until debate was past hope and the bill of abdication was offered to Parliament to vote upon. The members of Parliament had been elected by their constituents primarily to vote on taxation, unemployment, relief, and the like; but voting on the abdication of the King, however tragic, is like any other job, once the theory of government by representation is accepted.

In the last four generations of the royal Hanoverian House now called Windsor, each generation has swung, pendulum-like, away from the generation preceding. Queen Victoria's Victorianism produced King Edward VII's gay Edwardians, who produced King George V, who, as the ideal bourgeois gentleman, produced the former Prince of Wales's special set. Already, that group, in turn, has fathered King George VI and his staid circle. More than similar names joined the four monarchs together in twos; in accordance with Mendel's law, King Edward VIII inherited King Edward VII's characteristics. Unfortunately, closed carriages and *cabinets particuliers* were superseded by royal airplanes, which anyone could see in the sky, and by night clubs, where everybody could watch. Furthermore, though the tradition of a constitutional monarchy is supposed to produce kings "whose function is mediation, who have no policies of their own," it suddenly bred, to its shock, an individualist. No one knows what King Edward would have arrived at had he gone in chaos over the government's heads to the people's hearts. He is the most contemporary man England has known: his charm is cinematographic; though born to the purple, he has always had an inferiority complex. An exceptionally wise mind called him the *roi des humbles*. He has never liked the lords and ladies; he was emotionally drawn to the poor, perhaps because they supplied reality. As those who are new and on the way up are called *nouveaux riches*, King Edward, with his sympathies tending downward, was a strange and sad *nouveau pauvre*. Ever since he reached his manhood, it was known that he had no friends; he was content with the friendly faces around him. Through a democratic disequilibrium, he has been an escapist from his royal destiny. It is characteristic of his family and of the dangerous ironies binding them together today that his desired haven was marriage, even though in his family's eyes it was perhaps worse than his not being married at all. His ancestors were marrying men, and domestic. It was the public's delight to know that his father, George V, demanded that his wife, the Queen, be home at the palace to pour his afternoon tea.

Politically, the English are dualists in a manner formerly confined to metaphysics. With their rational mind, they empower democracy, but with their emotional imagination, they still give credit, perhaps wisely, to that miracle-loving element in human beings which tends toward iconography, kings, prophets, and special beings in strange, lovely garments. This element in other lands has recently found its less monarchic outlet in Nazi trappings, Fascist fanfares, a Communism which makes a shrine of Lenin's tomb, and, in America, a worship of cinema stars. King Edward has left the hierarchic for the romantic. He has been temporarily distrusted; it is possible that hereafter he will always be loved.

DECEMBER 23

London is facing not only a new year but a new king. If you didn't know the new King of England, you might think him "dry and not very human," according to the *Times*, whose task apparently is to keep kings in their place, in both senses of the phrase. George VI is moderately intelligent, is interested in details, lacks his father's quarter-deck manner but has inherited his appreciation of obedience, duty, rank, and work. Since he starts with the emotional support aroused by his brother's abdication, and without the unpopularity with which his father began his reign, it is now felt that George VI will actually prove to be an even more useful constitutional king than George V. The country does not want an inventive, brilliant monarch and is relieved that it isn't getting one. The stammer of which he was practically cured ten years ago doesn't occur in private but can occasionally make a painful pause in a public speech. He was the most fragile of the royal children, but is now the most athletic. He is a left-handed tennis player, and good enough to have once entered the Wimbledon championships. He is the only one of the family who is anything like as good a shot as his father, and he uses the same stiff-armed gunning style; he likes most to stalk deer. He took part in the Battle of Jutland as a naval officer. When he served at the naval station of Portsmouth, he was known as Dr. Johnson, because of some weighty remark he made. By his father's orders, he was shown no favors. It is part of the Hanoverian tradition for the fathers to be harsh with their sons.

The new Queen's family, the Bowes-Lyons, are heads of an ancient coal business with headquarters at Newcastle-on-Tyne; they also control the Marley Hill Chemical Company. Her father is the fourteenth Earl of Strathmore and Kinghorne. The young Queen drives her own car, adores fishing, hates foolish flattery, and thinks she hasn't much sense of humor. In Scotland, she is now called the Scotch Queen, though she was actually born at her parents' Hertfordshire seat. Scotland pays no attention to that. The Queen's mother traces her ancestry back to the fifteenth century; her father was a country parson.

When it seemed, during the crisis, as if they might become King and Queen, the Duke and Duchess of York, who are churchgoers, prayed that it wouldn't happen. It has happened. They have lost whatever privacy they once knew.

Owing to the bitter partisanship that colored it, the ex-King's abdication has produced a historic social upheaval. Ambitious individuals who for almost a year have been busily basking near the throne and the flat in Bryanston Court are now busy being turncoats. For a week the Cromwellian terms Roundhead and Cavalier resounded oddly through the Ritz. Now nearly the only Cavaliers left are Americans. With one prominent exception, most of the leading members of the Wallis Collection, as Mrs. Simpson's circle was called, have stood stanch. Never having been political-minded, these Americans have paradoxically stuck it out as king's men, have remained loyal to their compatriot, whom turncoats now pretend they never liked and hardly knew, and deserve credit.

The Archbishop of Canterbury's fulmination against the King's friends has irritated many and may lead to the BBCs (because it broadcast his words and the ex-King's farewell) being rebuked by Parliament for its forward participation in state affairs. Furthermore, since the Church only accidentally provoked the moral crisis about the King's private life—the bishop whose speech did the provoking stated that he was unaware any private life existed when he wrote his address—certain liberal minds feel the Church is as tardy in its moralizing as it was premature in its provoking. Also, the new divorce bill of A. P. Herbert is now coming up in Parliament for its last reading, and some amelioration—now that it's too late—of the Church's strict attitude toward the remarriage of divorced persons is hoped for, to clear an atmosphere in which divorce and remarriage have lately been perilously important. It is awkward that many Englishmen believe that the Church of England was established by Henry VIII because he wanted a divorce so that he might remarry.

Many now wonder what conditions of his youth and experiences of his adult life made Edward VIII decide to abdicate in order to marry for love. When he was young, it was reported that he had decided to refuse the throne. Labour sentiments and postwar utopian hopes then ran high; the throne was less popular than today. It is possible that he accepted the throne last year because he thought the time right for him as King to lead the country and do some good. Personal political acts, good or bad, are forbidden a constitutional monarch. Just as his grandfather was accused of royal intrusion when he tried to promote friendship between France and England, then pro-German, so Edward VIII was regarded with disfavor when, on this summer's extremely unofficial holiday, he saw Prince Paul of Yugoslavia; the Greek dictator, General Metaxas; and, lastly, Kemal Atatürk, whom he even told to come and visit him sometime. Finally, he unofficially went to see the Welsh unemployed. It was by these visits that he arrayed first the Foreign Office, then Parliament, against him, a discouraging combination. Helped by a king's-men party—there was a nucleus in Winston Churchill, Lords Beaverbrook and Rothermere, and Black Shirt Sir Oswald Mosley, who wanted to destroy Baldwin—a king bolder than the King might have tried Fascism to put his ideas through. A weaker king would never have had such ideas. Whatever it was he yearned to do (if anything, for no one is sure), King Edward was further hampered by lack of education. As a little boy, he didn't want to learn and, being obstinate, succeeded. To this day he is a nonreader. Thus the King of England matured with less knowledge of books than any Labour member in his House of Commons; in his House of Lords, few peers could have been so unfamiliar with the classics. Perhaps because men are suspicious of the female intellect, future queens are usually highly educated. At the age of ten, the Princess Elizabeth, as heiress presumptive, is learning to learn.

The Archbishops of Canterbury and York.

Semiofficial opinion now describes the result of the King Edward crisis as a waste rather than a loss. Yet whether he left his throne out of discouragement or a yearning for domesticity, or both, he took something with him that no one else had—a talent which the Bourbons considered the art of kingship, and which consists of the gift to charm his people, to arouse a nation's enthusiasm by the eye, the voice, the manner of the man. This now is indeed a waste. It is also a loss.

1937 Mme. Tussaud's famous waxworks has lately been running a modest advertisement in the newspapers which reads: "Dly. & Sun. (10-10). Portrait Model. Mrs. Simpson." The wax effigy of the lady from Baltimore is displayed on the second floor, on the line of march which leads the visitor a few feet later to the waxen figures of the Royal Family. It is the only unnumbered, uncatalogued, and isolated item in the whole show. Mrs. Simpson merely has her name on a card at her feet, isn't mentioned in the official booklet, and has a whole wall niche, with special lighting, to herself. She is shown in a scarlet evening gown, which the guard told us had been copied from one of her actual gowns; it seems the Tussauds are very strict about costuming. They have even equipped her with a Continental-looking handbag that bears her initials in rhinestones. The guard said that Mrs. Simpson hadn't posed for the figure, and so wasn't what the house calls "modeled from life," as, for instance, Hobbs, the famous Surrey cricketer, was, and Primo Carnera, whose bathrobed figure "is an accurate representation of his actual size." Mrs. Simpson was modeled from photographs, in haste, and set up about a fortnight after the abdication of King Edward. At first, the waxworks' visitors gathered in front of her dummy and said things, as if to her, but they no longer do that. All we heard when we were there was a little boy asking his parents who Mrs. Simpson was. His parents didn't say.

A few feet beyond her, and defended from her only by a group of Famous Soldiers in uniform, is the Royal Family. Two steps lead up to a dais on which King George VI and Queen Elizabeth are posed beneath a red velvet canopy. On the top step stand all the royal relatives—all, that is, except the Duke of Windsor. The morning after his abdication, his effigy, in its gold-frogged scarlet tunic, was removed from beneath the canopy and taken down two steps. It now stands on the floor, well over toward Mrs. Simpson. Even Lady Patricia Ramsay, the daughter of the Duke of Connaught, is closer to the canopy, and one level higher in the Tussaud world, than ex-King Edward VIII. On a pedestal just behind him is the Duke of Wellington, whose boot is even with the former ruler's neck.

It's all quite symbolic of the current reaction to the recent crisis. The two protagonists of December's Empire-shaking epic are now rarely recalled in London. The legend-making instinct inherent in humanity has, however, gone on to create rumors about other members of the unhappy Royal Family —fantastic stories which have been officially denied by at least one journal. It is now clear that the crisis had nothing to do with questions of government, but was entirely concerned (as its backwash today demonstrates) with social problems—such as whether divorce and remarriage are laic or clerical problems, whether one should unquestionably accept the Archbishop of Canterbury's recent appeal for a "recall to religion," and whether inhumane unemployment, such as King Edward deplored in Wales, can be prevented. There is also some question as to how much ex-royalty should reasonably cost. These are the real and undramatic crises of the English winter. The single dramatic crisis that led up to them has been forgotten, except by worldly, political minds that still wonder what effect it must eventually have on succeeding generations in the House of Windsor.

An unusual novel, *Nightwood*, by Djuna Barnes, was recently published here before its appearance in America. In an unsigned paragraph on the jacket, T. S. Eliot praises it as a book which "has nothing to offer to readers whose temperament attaches them to either an easy or a frightened optimism," and the not easily pleased *Sunday Times* eulogized the volume in a similar serious vein. It is a difficult book to describe, since the only proper way of dealing with its strange, nocturnal elements is to have written it in the first place, which surely no one but Miss Barnes could have done. Certainly only she would have so thoroughly and deliberately steeped herself in the eighteenth century in order to have conveniently at hand its richer vocabulary, and to grasp, without reaching too far across time, those early novel-patterns in which the amative, ribald, and melancholy states of man's mind were plot enough and to spare. The period of the book is 1925. The principal characters are a Viennese Jew who is posing as a baron; two American girls, one of whom becomes a hound of hell to the other, who is her doomed adorer; and a San Francisco-born Irishman, Dr. Matthew O'Connor. His fantastic monologues—the conversation becomes a dialogue only when his listener can squeeze a word in sidewise—are the pulse of the book. Sometimes he touches on subjects which have rarely been treated with such freedom. In his final oration, which he starts while on his sinful attic cot, and attired in a woman's nightgown and wig, he becomes an unforgettable spokesman for liars and lovers of all genders and generations.

Miss Barnes's verbal talent at times goes into a trance, then wakes again to phrases of amazing beauty. If you enjoy remarkable reading and writing, *Nightwood* is not to be missed.

After the longest ballyhoo and one of the shortest runs on record for an all-star mélange, Sir James Barrie's *The Boy David*, with Elisabeth Bergner, and sets by Augustus John, has closed. When Miss Bergner first appeared in London, she was likened to Bernhardt; as a little Peter Pan David who slew giants but was afraid to sleep in the dark, Miss Bergner displayed, according to critics, a naïveté which she could use to distraction "without ever being nauseating." These are words which no critic ever applied to Sarah Bernhardt. For that matter, they aren't words which David ever applied to himself in the Psalms.

MARCH 10

Since for the first time multitudes of Americans are coming to London for a coronation, the Americans might like to know what an English coronation ceremony actually consists of. Most of the English don't know, either. It is so complicated that of the eight thousand peers, peeresses, and notables who will be squeezed into Westminster Abbey, few will truly know what they are looking at—providing their seats let them see anything.

To begin with, all coronation ceremonies in Christian countries have Jewish elements based on the ritual Samuel used in anointing Saul King of Israel. Furthermore, English kings were for generations crowned according to a Saxon ceremony called Ethelred's Ritual, which was first used to crown King Edgar, in 973. A few hundred years later, owing to the Norman influence of William the Conqueror on the vanquished Saxons, something more modern was desired, and in 1307 the *Liber Regalis* was adopted. It is the manual largely followed in the crowning of English kings ever since, and with certain modifications, it will be used in 1937 to crown George VI.

According to W. J. Passingham, an English authority on coronations, the most important duty of the clergy on the coronation morning is to make sure that "the Ampulla be filled with Oil and, together with the Spoon," ready on the altar of Westminster Abbey. For it must be understood that in theory an English coronation is essentially a religious rite, and the sacred oil, when touched to the King's head, breast, and hands, supposedly endows him with a "spiritual jurisdiction and an inalienable sanctity," with divine approval thereafter taken for granted—points on which King Edward VIII and the Archbishop of Canterbury were definitely known not to see eye to eye. George VI, being a devoted churchgoer, will, it is felt, confirm the coronation's more pious meaning.

The following is, very briefly, what will take place during the three hours of the Westminster Abbey coronation ceremony on May 12: Entering through the west door, the King and Queen will mount a platform, called the Theatre, between the choir and the altar. The Archbishop of Canterbury, with the Lord High Chancellor, the Lord Great Chamberlain, and others, all in magnificent attire, will then walk to the four sides of the Theatre, east, south, west, and north, in order, and four times say, "Sirs, I here present unto you King George, the undoubted King of this Realm," and four times the people will answer, "God save King George the Sixth!" This is the Act of Recognition. Trumpets will then sound while noblemen who have been granted the traditional privileges present the Regalia—articles of temporal

Sir Winston Churchill—**History never diminished him even when it ignored him**.

and spiritual symbolism which figure dramatically in the coronation proce-
dure. The Regalia include the following: Saint Edward's Staff, which is made
of gold, and was reputed once to contain a fragment of the True Cross; the
Golden Spurs, which a peer touches to the King's heels in a feudal gesture;
the King's Royal Sceptre with the Cross, which is placed in the King's hand
during the coronation (it is pure gold, is studded with rubies and emeralds,
and in Edward VII's reign was adorned with the great Star of Africa, the
largest cut diamond in the world); the Pointed Sword of Temporal Justice   69

and the pointed sword of Spiritual Justice, both in red velvet scabbards tricked with fine gold and carried at the King's side as emblems of his just dealing with men; the Sword of Mercy, which is unscabbarded and blunt, and is carried before the Sovereign; the Jeweled Sword of State, which blazes with rubies, emeralds, and diamonds in the rose, thistle, and shamrock pattern, and which is valued at $1,000,000; the King's Sceptre with the Dove, which is of gold, and is an emblem of mercy; the King's Orb, which is placed in the King's right hand as he is crowned, and afterward carried in his left— a six-inch globe of gold, set with rubies, sapphires, and emeralds, and topped by a cross standing on a great amethyst; Saint Edward's Crown, the most important of the three State crowns, since it's the one the King is crowned with (it is of gold, with pearls and diamonds forming four crosses; the cap within is crimson velvet lined with taffeta, turned up with ermine); and the State Crown, made for Queen Victoria and containing the famous hen's-egg Black Prince ruby, to which, for George V's coronation, the second Star of Africa diamond was added. (Both of the Stars were cut from the great Cullinan diamond.) This is the crown the people will see the King wearing on his drive back to Buckingham Palace after the coronation. It is so heavy that the King is "eased of its weight" by his bishops during the Homage. While responses are sung by choirs, all this Regalia is laid on the altar.

Then begins the Communion Service. After the Sermon, the King will take the Oath, in which he swears to be merciful and just, and to support his clergy. After this the King—seated on the Coronation Chair, and covered by a silken canopy held by four Knights of the Garter, who afterward will keep the canopy as their traditional fee—will be anointed with oil. For this the King will remove his crimson Robe and Cap of State, so that his flesh may be touched. He will then be clothed in the Supertunica; the Golden Spurs will be touched to his heels; he will be girded with a sword by the Lord Great Chamberlain, and ungirded; he will be invested with the Armilla and the Royal Robe; he will be presented with the Orb; and the Wedding Ring of Marriage to the Church will be put on the fourth finger of his right hand. Just before the King is given the Sceptres with the Cross and the Dove, one in each hand, the Lord of Worksop Manor will draw a glove onto the King's hand (the Lord of Worksop Manor also has the honor of holding up the King's arm, by the elbow, lest he tire). Then the Archbishop will crown the King with Saint Edward's Crown. At that moment, all the peers will cover their heads with their coronets and all present will shout, "God save the King!" Outside, guns will be fired.

Following the Archbishop's exhortation and benediction, the King will be lifted onto his throne, and then at last will come the Homage. This starts with the Archbishop kneeling before his Sovereign, swearing to be faithful and true. If there were a Prince of Wales, he would then swear to be a "liege man of life and limb." There is talk of having little Princess Elizabeth, as Heiress Presumptive, speak this oath, but it probably will be delegated to someone else. When the Homage of clergy and peers is ended, all present will shout "as loudly as they may, 'May the King live for ever!'" Then they turn their attention to the Queen, who goes through a similar though briefer ceremony, after which both take Communion.

With such a ritual will King George VI and Queen Elizabeth be crowned, *Deo volente*, on May 12, in London.

The Coronation Chair in Westminster Abbey.

There should be an acute pulp-paper shortage in Europe soon, as at least one result of the plentitude of Coronation praises being printed in the newspapers here. An astrologer has predicted that the Coronation "might be badly mismanaged." Maybe that has been written in the stars, but it has been written nowhere else. England has in recent years been through financial doldrums and in recent months through constitutional pains. The Coronation means a new King and £20,000,000 to London. To both, the city, its press, and its people are loyally preparing an energetic and splendid welcome.

At the Ideal Home Exhibition, there is a Coronation piano (marked "Sold") with a white body and red and blue keys. In the shadow of the Exhibition's great gold effigy of King George VI there are, still unsold, bargain busts of King Edward VIII marked "1s. 6d., to Clear." In frivolity shops, where the display cards say "Little Satin Crowns Will Twinkle on Your

Coronation Lingerie," are chemises with the crown twinkling on one hip, brassières with it twinkling at the exact center, and corsets painted with the crown, the lion, and the unicorn, who shies up from the left hip. There are crowns on bath towels. There are veal galantines shaped like crowns, cold hams glazed with the royal cipher in green aspic. Once again this is a Georgian town.

King George VI came to the throne without preparation on December 11. On December 14, a courtier solemnly announced that within two days the new King had shown a vast improvement. What with all the sycophancy and the equally false belittling of the royal couple's qualities, it is being made difficult for the average Englishman to size up the true possibilities of the man whose character is far and away more important for the monarchy than that of any sovereign ever crowned in the past. By temperament, the King seems to be the type of person who should not be sequestered. As a human being, he could have placed himself advantageously in life on his own merits. Being self-conscious, he makes tentative dashes to promote ease in conversation; then, being modest, stifles the impulse. Asking impersonal questions and hearing about details are thus a relief to him. Being shy and comparatively inexperienced as a monarch, he still bungles the small social relations that aren't covered by formal protocol and are therefore his personal responsibility. For instance, it is hard for him to say good-by to people. This is hard on them, too, as by the rules of etiquette they can't leave till they are dismissed. He laughs especially at nonsense when people give him a chance, has a sense of fun rather than a sense of humor. His laughter comes out in an uncontainable burst and on a rather high note. His voice has a pleasing timbre; his accent has none of the qualities which in his older brother's case so shocked purists.

Probably his best personal equipment for not being swamped by his job is his capacity for detachment; he can separate himself from his métier. As he has said, he is not palace-minded. He likes a quiet weekend, which up to now he usually spent at the small Royal Lodge at Windsor, with his wife and two little daughters, who call him "Pàpa," not "Papà." There, all four would be active in the garden together from Friday till Monday. Princess Elizabeth had a small wheelbarrow and trundled light rubbish; the King pruned his shrubs. He and the Queen instituted a new tradition by not having either an equerry or a lady-in-waiting with them over the weekend. In an effort to check fashionable weekend flights from London, which he didn't approve of on principle, King George V usually stayed in town over Sunday, setting an example; Edward VIII invariably left it with a large party, setting the pace; the new King likes his family, his country, and his peace.

No one knows what notions of real life the King may have. One of his brothers once said that as children they were alternately told they were very ordinary little boys indeed and not to forget that they were princes. From this confusing adolescent training the King has grown into a singularly unaffected man, quicker than people think and say. He is morally solid, physically nervous, and has a sharp temper which may prove to be his salvation in his new position as a modern monarch whom the people will tend to enslave. At the moment, and before the wear and tear of his public post alter

Windsor Castle.

him, the King has the mannerisms, the reluctance, the mixture of hauteur and consideration that are the result of the highest English breeding. No one knows how the future will stylize him—whether as a distinct character or as a piece of national property, whether he will fit the picture or make his own portrait. In either case, he will unquestionably be very popular— and very soon. When he is seen in the ordinary way here, wearing a derby, what the common people invariably say, in a kind of thoughtful concurrence, is " 'E's got a nice face."

MAY 5

Whatever else may be final about it, this will certainly be the last equestrian Coronation. Anyhow, that is the opinion of the postillions in the Buckingham Palace stable yard. For King George V's Coronation procession the stables furnished three hundred royally owned and trained horses; for King George VI's, they can muster only a hundred and twenty. Even for princes, horseflesh is being replaced by petrol fumes, which are cheaper. In 1919, for economy, King George V disposed of the famous Hanoverian creams, which were used only to draw the State Coach at a Coronation or an opening of Parliament. The first of them had been given to Queen Victoria by her uncle King Leopold I of the Belgians. These pink-eyed, so-called

Overleaf: "On May 12, London rose at four-thirty . . . and watched George VI's magnificently colored Coronation procession."

73

ponies (they stood only fifteen hands high) were an exclusive family possession. They were bred in England for forty years, and were never gelded. The mares remained in the paddock; only the stallions appeared in processions. When the stud was broken up, the younger stallions were given to various regiments as drum horses, and further breeding was prohibited.

In 1936, for economy, King Edward VIII closed the stables at Windsor Castle where the fourteen Windsor grays resided and sent the animals to Buckingham Palace. The grays are mostly geldings. The lead hand horse, a mare named Angela, will be paired with Silver Fox (called Dawey in private life). He will be ridden by the head Royal Postillion in charge of the eight horses which will draw the magnificent four-ton twenty-two-carat gold-leafed State Coach (built for our George III) which the sixth George will ride in to and from his crowning. The vehicle carries neither coachmen nor footmen; at such moments, royalty rides alone. A King usually has four footmen, a Prince three; any other member of the Royal Family has two footmen. The state harness comes in both red and blue leather, with the metal parts gold-plated, and each set weighs a hundred and twenty-eight pounds. It was originally made for Queen Victoria's Diamond Jubilee. On Coronation Day, the horses will wear braided in their manes twenty-two yards of red or blue satin dressing. It takes two hours to prepare each animal. The seventy Royal Cleveland bays which will be in the procession are coach horses. Some of the Cleveland bays have white legs; these will be larded and stained with lampblack, so that they'll match the black-legged majority. Training for the Coronation in the Palace's little riding academy consists of having stableboys blow trumpets, whack drums, shoot guns, and wave their arms while the horses are ridden full tilt into flags and dummy figures suspended on pulleys. The dummies are dressed as soldiers, and one of them wears a bearskin, since green horses shy at a bearskin. Dummies in uniform are preferred to dummies in mufti because the horses must learn to go close to sentries, who, if royalty is in the arriving carriage, stand fearlessly close at present arms. The cost of a Royal Postillion's state livery of gold-embroidered scarlet jacket, gold spurs, white buckskin breeches and gloves, black velvet cap, white wig, black boots with flesh tops, and, on his right calf, a blue or red morocco leg guard to keep the off horse from sweating on his boot, comes to about £120. The horses at Buckingham Palace live in green-tiled stalls in a mews built by the great architect Nash, are fed four times a day with a chaff of corn and bran, and at night are given meadow or clover hay to pick over.

Being dressmaker to a new Queen is considered a great honor. Queen Elizabeth's magnificent Coronation robe and gown, which are to be embroidered with real gold thread, are being made up by Handley-Seymour of New Bond Street. About three dozen of her spring and summer costumes are being done in Bruton Street by Norman Hartnell, who is thirty-three, handsome, comes from Devonshire, and was educated at Cambridge. His costumes for The Footlights (the Cambridge equivalent of the Princeton Triangle Club) pleased Lady Duff-Gordon, who encouraged him to become a professional dressmaker. This he did ten years ago, in association with his sister and three assistants; today he has five hundred employees. Near the forest of Windsor he owns an exquisitely restored Regency country house—Lovel Dene—with

"God Save King George VI!" Acknowledging the cheers of the crowd from the balcony of Buckingham Palace: the Royal Family.

a swan-motived drawing room, superb old crystals, and a fine collection of faïence, his Rockingham-ware mauve cottages being especially precious.

When it was first suggested that the Queen be dressed by him, Her Majesty is said to have replied, "Oh, I'm not smart enough." It is known that up to the time she became Queen her Scotch maid, Kathleen, unwillingly advised the Duchess about her wardrobe. Being a Queen entails stricter sartorial duties, such as three hours and a half of fittings at Windsor Castle, in the course of which the Hartnell fitters were given tea and sent by the Queen out on the balcony to get a fine view of the changing of the guard. Dressing, for a young Queen, is difficult in England, where mature Queens have long been the favorites. If a young Queen fails to achieve an Alexandran elegance, she discourages the smart London peeresses; if she is too Frenchily chic, she antagonizes the suburbs.

Suburban ladies feel that they understand Queen Elizabeth. They probably err. To their way of thinking, to be the Queen would be ideal. By other people, it is known that Queen Elizabeth earnestly hoped that circumstances would not draw her and her husband onto England's great and difficult throne.

The whole complicated structure of the Empire, political, patriotic, emotional, and financial, was unquestionably badly shaken on December 11, 1936. Considering that damage, it is reckless of certain Londoners to regard the Coronation as a gilded, exhausting show put on merely to dazzle visitors from the Empire. The duty of everyone is to see clearly these days. Since the Statute of Westminster of 1931, all that has bound the Empire to England is the Crown, from which rich items could conceivably be lost, as hastily set exotic jewels often are. Without its now voluntary Empire, England would be only a small island off the west coast of Europe. One hears disparate rumors—that the Duke of Windsor will be the first President of the United States of Great Britain; also that he will never dare set foot again on English soil. What one will unquestionably hear on Coronation Day, as the superb Royal Coach winds through the throngs of English voters lining the streets, will be the cry "Long live the King!," shouted by a people who, more than at most Coronations, passionately hope it will come true.

MAY 16

On May 12, London rose at four-thirty, provided it had not already been on the sidewalks all the night before, and watched George VI's magnificently colored Coronation procession. It was composed of remarkable relics and innovations—costumes, coaches, soldiery, and a royal family, all brought up to date in the person of an ermine-caped young King whose sacred, ancient oaths, hesitantly sworn to before God and an Archbishop, had just been broadcast through loudspeakers to the whole world. It was a sight which no one who saw it well can ever forget. Three-quarters of the parade was made up of men whose profession is the bearing of arms, yet their costumes featured frogged tunics, aigrettes, bearskins, leopard pelts, kilts, striped turbans, scarlet coats, plaid pantaloons, gilt cuirasses, and waving plumes—all the pageantry of impracticability wherein England's genius for poetry and empire equally thrive. The culmination of the procession was as great a surprise as if the fabulous gold coach and its occupants had not been expected. Dominated by the motionless figure of the King, the coach was the perfect symbolic vehicle for constitutional monarchy, triumphantly and lovingly restored to its former prestige.

The House of Hanover's sixth George had Coronation music, the finest heard in centuries, dominated by the great Tudor and Stuart tunes of Byrd and Purcell. The clear clamor of the trumpets, the high sopranos of the boys in the choir, the Westminster scholars' *"Vivat"*'s, the Biblical verbiage of the ritual, in which well-coped clergy admonished at length a monarch reduced to a simple white shirt and breeches, made an unexpected emotional impression on listeners sensible of the ancient delinquencies and fresh hopes in this paradoxically monarchical democratic island. People of all classes, and people not easily moved today by fine phrases, fine music, hysteria, or faith, actually cried before the radio when the King, with those caesuras which are his controls in his difficult speech, swore, "All this I promise—to do." If its democratic Parliament, which alone can do anything, can raise faith equal to that which England has just put in its new King, who can do nothing, England is approaching one of those good times long since due her. The other three-quarters of this troubled globe wish her well.

A touch of London, viewed from Saint James's Park.

Since the eve of the Coronation, London's best celebrations have been nocturnal. Once the lights go on, the city turns out. Coronation Wednesday has flowed into Whitsunday in a continuous, fantastic floodlit rout for the *polloi,* and Palace balls, costume fetes, and state dinners on precious plate for the grandees. By the special traffic signs, one can tell what's going on, whether one is invited or not. The sign at Hyde Park Corner the night of Buckingham Palace's royal party read, "The Coronation Court Ball. Keep straight on." Piccadilly is nightly barricaded to everything except pedestrians by wooden doors and the street-traffic sign "The Coronation. No entry. Floodlighting." Everything public or private with half a claim to municipal beauty is floodlit till midnight. The Tower of London, illuminated for the first time in history, is a superb sight dead knights would die again to see. Westminster Abbey, the Admiralty, the Horse Guards, Saint Paul's, Wren's churches, the flowers in Saint James's Park—all are illuminated each night, and are nightly circled by shuffling, unwearying feet. Traffic is shunted so that you are bound to drive to floodlighting though you may have wanted to drive darkly among Hyde Park's empty tents and trees. At each traffic vortex, a police-car loudspeaker declaims, "Pedestrians! Do not pass before moving vehicles. The traffic will shortly be held up for you." No car honks. The packed streets are quiet except for the sound of tongues and feet, or shouts emerging from pubs open by special dispensation until midnight. In pubs, the crowds sing "Land of Hope and Glory" and American swing songs, drink His Majesty's health, and occasionally cheer for a brother over the water whom they toast as King Teddy.

According to a special apparatus installed in Whitehall for the procession, Queen Mary got eighty-five decibels of cheer from the crowd; the young King and Queen, eighty-three; some popular street-sweepers, seventy-six. Princess Juliana of Holland got seventy-three. A. P. Herbert was the only member of Parliament to use the privilege of arriving for the Coronation via the Thames in a private barge. Thomas Cook & Son are reported to have paid over £10,000 to descendants of the Duke of Wellington for permission to erect viewing stands around Apsley House, once a grateful nation's gift to the Iron Duke. The bus strike, the police orders requiring the public to be in place for the Coronation by 5:00 a.m., the London weather man's prediction of rain, the Wall Street slump, and King Edward's abdication are blamed for having kept a half-million people from the new King's show. The film of the Coronation itself and the procession that followed was a disappointment. As now shown here, after being censored by the Archbishop of Canterbury and the Duke of Norfolk, it consists of ten minutes of the King, principally riding in his coach. The English historical sense should have demanded at least a half hour of events that took a day to live through. Furthermore, the picture lacks some views of the small Princess who may have to do it all by herself someday, and, above all, gives an inadequate portrayal of that lady who, merely as a widowed consort, supplied a regal stability during the crisis—Queen Mary. The decibels of the cheering for her properly indicated what is here her high state.

May 26

It is ironic that Lord Snowden, who contended that strikes were obsolete, should die during a busmen's strike. Never has a transportation strike, which should have affected masses of holidaying people, been so ignored. It isn't rare for a populace to congregate by thousands in a capital's streets the night after a big show, but to congregate for seven nights—from Coronation Tuesday through Whitmonday—by millions and walk home each night, after tramping about for hours, is extraordinary. When Piccadilly Circus became hopelessly jammed that Sunday night, police loudspeakers generously announced, "Ladies and gentlemen, the Circus is yours." Considering the distress among the poor of London, it is surprising that no political heckler thereupon asked for bread.

To certain foreign visitors with egalitarian ideas, the devotion here of most Left Wing political parties to the monarchy is puzzling. Certainly the *Daily Herald*, morning Labour newspaper, printed more pictures of the Coronation than even the Conservative gazettes did. And in the Sunday-morning *People*, Hannen Swaffer, well-known Leftist columnist, deplored, in an emotional paragraph, that the Archbishop of Canterbury had cut from the official Abbey film the view of Queen Mary shedding tears ("Queen Mary had seen her eldest son abdicate . . . had seen the Throne saved because of the coolness of the British people.") and went on to say, "When you see the Coronation film I hope you will see not only the Royalty, the State coach, the glass-lined carriages . . . but the soldiers who came from all over the Commonwealth." To anyone familiar with the fierceness of Leftist French writers, who not only would put The People in capital letters but would probably try to jail any columnist who praised an imperial army or throne even in small letters, the English Reds' rosy liberalism is a pleasant puzzle. There are few such enigmas of civilized tolerance, let alone nonclass love, evident in Europe today.

Now that it's all over, it's admitted that such abnormalities as Abdications and Coronations are bad for English business. For three weeks before the Coronation, loyal people were too excited to buy, and during Coronation week were too patriotic to open shop and sell, even when they could. However, while coming-out parties won't help factories in Manchester or coalpits in Wales, there are now scheduled sixty-two elaborate balls for debutantes, who will furnish a June and July crop which the luxury trades will gratefully harvest. The Coronation itself has brought about exceptional State and social functions which are creating on all sides a revival of the great English hospitable manner. A Court Ball at Buckingham Palace led off the official post-Coronation season, with the new King and Queen dancing, not the customary opening classic quadrille, but a fox trot—though, to be sure, with different partners. Young Crown Prince Michael of Rumania was allowed to sit up late and watch. There have also been two State Banquets at the Palace in one week. The Speaker of the House of Commons, Captain the Right Honourable Edward Algernon FitzRoy, and his wife held a reception for royalty, Dominion officials, and bishops in vivid purple evening clothes. At 10 Downing Street, where Britannia really does her ruling of the waves today, Premier and Mrs. Baldwin gave a little dinner for the King and Queen. Mr. and Mrs. Anthony Eden entertained, for the benefit of Foreign Affairs, and Ambassador von Ribbentrop also held a reception, probably for the restoration of German colonies. The Papal Legate to the Coronation (who, as his Church has not yet recognized England's Protestant Reformation, was obliged to remain outside Westminster Abbey during the crowning of the English King) was tendered a fashionable reception to meet other highly placed clerics. The Tudor country home of the Duke and Duchess of Sutherland was opened for visitors from the Dominions and the Colonies, and hundreds arrived, including the Alake of Abeokuta under a gold umbrella of state.

In the poor districts of London, the children were given what New York calls block parties and London calls street teas, with tea, jam, and buns set on tables in the middle of the street and paid for by neighborhood penny subscriptions. Usually a sidewalk artist contributed colored chalk portraits of Their Majesties, God Bless Them. On such streets there were more Union Jacks and Long May They Reigns aflutter than in the smarter sections of London, devoted to the flag of Saint George and window boxes of red, white, and purple cineraria. The great political clubs went in for dignified Georgian decorations of crowns; ermine tails, painted on linen drapes; and comely red and blue, with gold laurel climbing fluted columns.

Along the Thames, where warships lay before the King reviewed the fleet at Spithead, pubs and other sailor haunts bore banners with the words "We All Love Jack Tar." Twenty thousand nonseafaring enthusiasts booked 81 train and boat passage to go to Portsmouth after breakfast, cruise down the line of a hundred and sixty ships, see the searchlight display that night, and get back to London around 4:00 a.m. England is an island, and England's Navy, especially since the European world has not turned out to be a better place to live in, is again of increasing importance.

JUNE 2

London is supposed to tolerate music, but not to want too much of it. The Coronation season has furnished a lot. Toscanini's six BBC concerts have thus far been so popular (and at such prices) that counterfeit tickets have been issued by unmusical crooks. Covent Garden has imported, for the most bejeweled opera audience left in Europe, Continental troupes—German, Italian, and French. For the first time, troupes from the Opéra and the Comique were invited to cross the Channel. Two performances of the *Ring* under Furtwängler have been included—one with Frida Leider, the other with Flagstad. However, the most curious operas have been those at Glyndebourne, where Mr. John Christie is for Mozart and Sussex what King Ludwig II was for Wagner and Bavaria. Christie's private opera house, fantastically set down in the midst of an otherwise empty rural landscape, offers that combination of eccentricity, wealth, and musical taste which has been the perquisite of occasional cultivated monarchs, usually called mad.

Christie is a sensible businessman who, to inherit the family fortune, had to prove he could earn his living, which he did by teaching chemistry at Eton, running a greengrocer's shop, and operating hotels. He is still a building contractor, and a manufacturer of movie-palace pipe organs. His specialty, though, is Mozart operas, out of which he fabricates a six-week season on his magnificent country estate, to which music lovers, by train, bus, and motor, have trekked in such numbers as to make this, Glyndebourne's fourth season, a sellout. It opened with a truly first-rate *Don Giovanni* preceded by the spectacle of the audience, in elaborate evening garb, promenading in the late-afternoon sunlight through fine walled gardens, circling the irised lake, and strolling across the acres of civilized lawn, their silhouettes, in colored silks and black broadcloth, theatrical against hills populated only by buttercups and larks. Christie's superb theory is that of a German *Residenz-Theater*; he houses a collection of able artists and musicians who from April to July will live nothing but Mozart in the middle of the Sussex downs. The arrangements for the audiences are remarkable: a loudspeaker in the cabbage patch to call chauffeurs in from the meadow car park; dressing rooms in which belated businessmen can hustle into their evening togs; and for the entr'acte suppers, a fine cellar of rare German wines, with a classical Greek tag for each vintage on the wine card. A quotation from Homer accompanies the twenty-three-shillings-a-bottle 1933 Forster Kirchenstück Riesling, Spätlese, Weingut Dr. Deinhard, Deidesheim.

The drawings of James Thurber at the Storram Gallery have been a rival attraction to the show of Constable's works at the Tate Gallery. It seems worth recording that Thurber has been appreciated as "Strindbergian" by the *New Statesman*, that he possesses "night-mare logic" for the *Sketch*, that

The Duke and Duchess of Windsor on their wedding day.

his "satire is allusive rather than logical" to the scholarly *Spectator*, and that—final triumph, from the *Observer*—his "drawings seem most satisfactorily funny when his captions are not. . . . Mr. H. G. Wells, even as a draughtsman, has a more complete humor than Thurber." Not so replete, though, as the unconscious *Observer*'s.

This is the season for London's charity balls, equally important for healthy rich and sick poor. Public hospitals here are maintained not by the municipality, but by gifts, an arrangement known as the Voluntary System. Till recently, many charity functions were rackets which socially profited the newly rich and financially aided charity organizers to the tune of from 12 to 15 per cent. Lately there has been a rebellion, with the big charity balls taken over by disinterested rich women with a notion of civic duty. There are three great annual charity balls on which thousands of lives depend: Saint Thomas's Hospital Ball, run by the Duchess of Marlborough; Queen Charlotte's Hospital Ball, which is a classic for country debs; and, most important, the Derby Ball, which has just been held in Grosvenor House with Lady Milbanke and Mrs. James Field as chairwomen. It was given for the benefit of the Royal Northern Hospital's maternity ward and was attended by the Duke and Duchess of Gloucester. One million and a half of the King's subjects in the populous Holloway district are the hospital's responsibility, and for that night the Duke's, in a way; for at such functions Royalty is a hard-working attraction. The other attraction for the ultra-fashionable gathering was the singing of Libby Holman.

Balletomanes will be touched to know that a Nijinsky Matinée, featuring Lord Berners' *Degas Ballet*, was held at His Majesty's Theatre in an effort to raise funds to maintain the unhappy Waslaw Nijinsky in his Swiss nursing home. This charity was sponsored, fittingly, by Lady Juliet Duff, whose mother, the Marchioness of Ripon, was influential in first bringing Nijinsky to Covent Garden in *Les Sylphides*. In those days, it was the public which was mad—over his grace.

For different reasons, the English Royal Family and the American newspaper editors were probably the parties most interested in the Duke of Windsor's wedding. London as a whole cared little; it did its caring about romance last December. Since then, whether through fate, poor advice, or plain ignorance of public psychology, the former favorite, ex-King Edward VIII, has, detail by detail, château by château, lost love and ground at home. Even the harsh decision which permitted neither Court friends nor his own kin to attend the wedding has elicited only one editorial protest and nearly no private complaints. Some external issues have aided his eclipse: the unexpected Coronation hit made by his understudy, King George VI; the solid farewell sentiment for Baldwin; and perhaps three books—Hector Bolitho's *King Edward VIII*, Geoffrey Dennis's *Coronation Commentary*, and, more pertinent and important, *The Magic of Monarchy*, by the *New Statesman*'s Kingsley Martin. But mostly the Duke has tragically arranged for his own decline. His Austrian pastimes of playing games and the bagpipes, and never reading a book; his postdivorce, prenuptial hurrying to his fiancée in France;

Alicia Markova and Anton Dolin in *Les Sylphides*.

his press photos posed to prove their happiness; his sharing with her, in the face of his sincere sympathy for the poor, the services of a £10-a-trip Paris coiffeur; above all, his playing in a golf match the day his brother received England's crown, and the selection of his father's birthday for a marriage whose incipient stages are reported to have hurried King George V's end—these, even more than his abdication, have cost the former King his country.

JUNE 23

The news that All Hallows, one of Sir Christopher Wren's famous City churches, is to be destroyed in the interest of progress has provoked the customary fine, futile protest here. In 1694, when the church was built, it was in Lombard Street; today it's in the backyard of a Barclays Bank. Few people ever set foot in the church, since it's hard to find; it's usually locked, and anyhow the City is busy worshiping money. More than any other country, England makes a fetish of parts of its past. As a suitable background for the almost intemperate monarchial fervor now sweeping the English public and press, and apparently even the Royal Family, the conservation of London's noble ancient architecture, civic or ecclesiastic, has become a peculiar contemporary necessity. London's Tudor architecture was destroyed in the Great Fire of 1666; its eighteenth- and nineteenth-century great classic building is being destroyed by men in the twentieth. It should be noted that a form of courtly life has been razed, in the past few years, along with certain of the city's most shapely elderly architectural designs—Pembroke, Lansdowne, Devonshire, and Chesterfield houses, and the mansions lining Berkeley, Grosvenor, and Portman squares, where decorous linear unity was integral to the civic scheme, and carefree new apartment houses now protrude. Bedford Square, the only one of the handsome Bloomsbury units to remain intact today, tomorrow will probably lose its east side to the British Museum, which, to shelter older things, wants to destroy beauty already sufficiently mature. Sir Joshua Reynolds' Leicester Square house has been demolished so that the Automobile Association can have larger premises; Curzon Street's little gem, Crewe House, is today being carved up for bus-company offices. At the recent razing of the Adam brothers' exquisite Adelphi Terrace, there was such outcry that the buyer's name was withheld from the public. Signal nineteenth-century losses include Rennie's remarkable Waterloo Bridge, doomed by the Labour party that was the intellectual's hope. Nash's Regent Street and Quadrant, part of his precocious city plan, are gone, and his Regent's Park has lost one of its last three isolated and pedimented cream-colored mansions—Saint Dunstan's, formerly a home for blind soldiers, which Countess Haugwitz-Reventlow, formerly Miss Barbara Hutton, has just torn down. She is building a quite nice red-brick house in its place.

What is causing London's disfigurement is, naturally, what caused its former beauty—money. Rates and taxes on a great town house are £5,000 yearly. Despite the amazing number of very rich English—almost as astonishing as the incredible quantity of extremely poor English—the grand old style must slow down under modern taxes, heavier here than anywhere else on earth. As encouragement to razing good old buildings and erecting new, shoddy ones, building societies recently offered 90- instead of the usual

75-per-cent coverage and flat owners now demand up to 10 per cent instead of down to the 5 per cent which used to be house rental's profit. As for churches, the Archbishop of Canterbury had them excluded from the Ancient Monuments Act by declaring the Church could properly manage its own treasures. It has tried to. The Diocese of London, whose City sites are worth pecks of money, has since 1920 tried to sell eighteen churches, which have been saved by societies ironically "representing the interests of history, architecture, and proper sentiment." Liveliest of these bodies is Lord Esher's Society for the Protection of Ancient Buildings, founded in 1877 by William Morris, John Ruskin, Thomas Carlyle, and friends. While the Society has worked to save oddments such as beamed pubs, Saxon rubble, and bell cages, thus aiding in the revival of campanology among bellpullers all over the island, it has mainly fought to save England's great Renaissance architecture from a Church- and Victorian-minded public inclined to revere only British Gothic. The Society is now also saving windmills. Its pamphlet reproduces a little windmill, "drawn from memory or imagination" by the Duke of Windsor when a child of eight.

George VI's new reign, rain or shine, continues in a kaleidoscope of colorful processions, uniforms, scarlet-coated Guardsmen, levees, and Royal Family appearances at private and public functions to a degree not hitherto seen. For Ascot, the King had a hundred and thirty-two guests, which was an unprecedented number. At the Trooping the Colour, behind handsome historic

Changing of the Royal Guard at Buckingham Palace.

Whitehall, he was exceptionally accompanied by a full royal escort of Household Cavalry. His birthday, which is really December 14, has been, also exceptionally, changed forever to June 9 for official celebration. At Windsor, for the first time in twenty-three years, there was held a service of the Most Noble Order of the Garter, of which the two Queens are the only lady members. They wore the same blue velvet robes as the Knights, but with slightly smaller heron-plumed hats. In Saint George's Chapel, the Duke of Windsor's banner hung in fourth, no longer in first, place, its heraldry charged with a silver label of "difference," charged in turn with the crown he has laid down.

The greatest of the governmental pageants were the eight nocturnal Coronation Tattoos held in the floodlit green fields of Aldershot, with a mixture of fifty cavalry and infantry regiments, artillery brigades, and signal and tank corps. At the second performance alone, seventy-seven thousand people were present. They sat uncovered through a cloudburst, cheered everything in sight, sang "Cockles and Mussels, Alive, Alive-O!," and saw their army give a superb theatrical performance which for costume, music, color effects, and what looked like a gigantic male ballet maneuvering in fancy clothes was probably unique among the armament programs of Europe today. Twenty-four massed bands played the Coronation March from Meyerbeer's *Le Prophète* for the slow marching. Military apparel all the way from Tudor knights in armor through Charles I pikemen to the Duke of Wellington's foot soldiers was displayed in dramatized historical tableaux, the best being "the Raising of the Seaforth Highlanders" (in person), with torches, and seven kilted pipe bands skirling "Loch Duich." The sole modern reality was supplied by "a Modern Battle Action" of tanks and khaki-clad gunners. We can only say that as a demonstration calculated to comfort (or scare to death) the civilian population, it wasn't a patch on Herr Hitler's annual Nürnberg summer displays, in which thousands, not hundreds, of tanks and soldiers make mimic war; mock villages are really bombed; cannons truly deafen; and planes strafe German recruits as accurately as if they were Allied troops. England should be happy that its Aldershot show is thus inferior to those across the North Sea.

JUNE 30

Three great-grandchildren of Queen Victoria—the Duke of Kent, the Marquess of Milford Haven, and Lord Louis Mountbatten—were present at the Lyric Theatre's historic first-night presentation of Laurence Housman's hitherto banned play, *Victoria Regina*. Owing to a recent decision that "one hundred years after the accession of a deceased sovereign, the sacredness of his or her character has sufficiently diminished to allow of stage presentation," the play opened on June 21, one hundred years and one day, to the dot, after Queen Victoria first mounted the British throne. The curtain speech which the author told the unbelievably distinguished audience he was not allowed to make was to have begun as follows: "Your Royal Highnesses, my lords, ladies and gentlemen, at last!—thanks mainly, I believe, to the gracious and unusual common sense of his late Majesty King Edward,

Pamela Stanley as Queen Victoria and Carl Esmond as Prince Albert in *Victoria Regina*.

to whom, now Duke of Windsor, I tender my grateful thanks. . . ." It is ironic that of the various iconoclasms King Edward tried to inaugurate in his brief reign, this one, of freeing his family's private life for public presentation, should alone succeed—after he was in exile.

In this final production of his major opus, Mr. Housman's long martyrdom to censorship takes a rest. For thirty-five years Housman has been having his plays banned because they were always about either the Royal or the Holy Family. In 1902, his *Bethlehem* was refused a license because it dealt with the Nativity, and years later his *Pains and Penalties* was banned because it dealt with the domesticity of King George IV and Queen Caroline. Having recently deleted what, even years ago, was considered that royal drama's most horrific line—"Heirs male of the last generation have not been a conspicuous success"—Housman now announces that the Lord Chamberlain will license the play for public production by whoever wants to take the risk. Both these plays, as well as parts of *Victoria Regina*, have, of course, already been presented here at what are called—and are not—private theatres, where anyone may see the show by buying a ticket plus a membership in the society rigged up for the production of, and usually candidly named after, the play in question.

While the London stage could do with less censorship, and even none might seem suitable in a country calling itself (when not cheering for the King) a democracy, nevertheless what the theatre here needs more than liberty is good plays. The theatrical season which opened last autumn is now closing in summer on its first warranted important hit: *Victoria Regina*. Had Queen Victoria acceded a few months earlier in 1837, the 1937 spring theatrical season would have been better off.

The other matter of censorship—for once, on your side of the water—has been the banned Paramount newsreel of Chicago police beating up the steel strikers, which is now being shown to spectators so horrified that the film should probably have been banned here, too. There is no sequence in its scenes, merely a muddle of massed clubbing, of untidy, ill-directed brutality, of inert fallen forms; the commentator's loud, overdramatic drone also helped to confuse. At the movie house where we saw the film, it was followed by the old Silly Symphony "Who Killed Cock Robin?," in which the police birds beat all the other birds. For once, no one laughed at Mr. Disney.

With the Church, whether Roman or Anglican, being alternately hectored first on the Rhine, then on the Thames, the last straw for Catholics here has been the discovery that the Bilbao boatload of four thousand Basque Catholic children recently welcomed as refugees are neither Basques nor Catholics. Whereas only fifty of the youngsters were originally rated as non-Catholic, actually twenty-four hundred of them have turned out to be not only not Catholics but positive infidels, having been brought up without any religion whatever. Furthermore, they aren't Basques but Asturians, Galicians, and Castilians. Indeed, the only thing which the Basque Catholic children were supposed to be and really are is children. Like children, they have run away from the hostels to which they have been sent, have learned to say "O.K." under the impression that it is English, and with the heartbreaking illogic of childhood, stoned the radio which announced the fall of Bilbao.

Considering its patient nonsectarianism, both religious and political, the Salvation Army has felt nothing but the sharp tooth of ingratitude at its Congress Hall, in Clapton, where its three hundred and fifty Spanish children were regarded by the neighborhood as "prisoners." Something like friendly jailbreaks were hospitably organized for picnics on the Hackney Marshes, and Salvation lassies, out hunting the runaways, had to be protected by policemen.

The confusion reigning not only among foreign children but among European adults is generally apparent here in London, today the Continental clearinghouse for diplomacy as well as for exiles. There's more talk in select circles of spies and secret agents than has been heard since the war. Russia's arrests and executions; the murder of the anti-Fascist Rosselli brothers in France; Germany's increasing passion about nonintervention, priests, food, and nonfree speech; Italy's problems of Anglophobia, her dead in Spain, and sick finance may all be merely news of Europe in New York, but can be news of friends here. Any German, Russian, or Danubian at a cocktail party thinks every other German, Russian, or Danubian is an informer; suspicion and propaganda, both innocent and professional, run neck and neck. The League of Nations' failure to decide what, as regards Europe, people should think has resulted in innocent people trying to think for themselves, with violent results; the existence of dictatorships has revived the secret agent, the *salon* professional propagandist unemployed in republican regimes.

JULY 7

Now that the so-called Eleven Royal Weeks' celebration of the Coronation, from May 5 to July 22, is drawing to an end, it's not too early to remark that the only unusual public feature about the Coronation Season has really been the Coronation. All the other big events—Ascot, the Derby, the military Tattoos, the International Horse Show at Olympia, the Hendon Air Show—have been in pageantry and popularity what they are in any prosperous year, the word "Coronation" being the only difference in the programs. The King and Queen have made the regular expected—and the customary unexpected—appearances normal to a recently crowned young couple who are still news. Public activities of the rest of the Royal Family have been given only that intelligent, slight acceleration natural after government has received a shock. The season, in pomp, has been like all other seasons except those two lean ones when King George V was ill and when King Edward VIII was willful. Nothing has changed.

Seven months ago England saw shaken to their foundations her four most powerful institutions—the Crown, the Church, Parliament, and the press. And again nothing has changed. It's impossible for a foreigner—an American, a Frenchman, a Chinaman—to understand the English from his foreign viewpoint. He's got to try to understand them from the English viewpoint, which is nearly impossible, it being composed of local picturesque traditions observed as seriously as if they were universal scientific laws; a certain view of undeviating duty which, though it has been vaguely transplanted all over the Empire, flourishes best as a strictly island growth; and a combination of painstaking sentimentality and thumping realism, both drawn on in emergency as interchangeably as if they were the same thing. These disparate elements provoked, as well as pulled England through, the four-faceted December crisis, apparently without a scratch. Only time and the progressing history of other nations will tell if some remaining scars might not have been a healthier, more sensitive sign.

Of the four institutions, the Church has been hardest hit by criticism. The Archbishop of Canterbury is overwhelmingly the most unpopular man in England. Nor has his recent stand in the House of Lords on the bitterly needed and debated new and easier Divorce Bill helped. Considering his positivisms of December and June on the topic, his late admission that since, as a churchman, he couldn't support divorce (which, as a citizen, he had to admit was permitted by law), he wouldn't vote at all sounded like casuistry. The disarray among his Bishops on the Divorce Bill question was also illuminating. While the Bishop of Saint Albans was against divorce for anybody, the Bishop of Durham was against the Bishop of Saint Albans—for probably not having even read the Divorce Bill—and was against the Archbishop of Canterbury for not accepting the authority of Saint Matthew on divorce. The Archbishop of York was for the Bill as a law, but against the Bishops' voting for it, as they are upholders of public morals. The Bishop of Birmingham, always so modern that he has sometimes been called an atheist, was for the Bill, and even for the Church's remarrying innocent divorced parties. England has always feared the political influence of clerics, smelling in it papacy, yet has made its Anglican bishops Lords Spiritual, who, ranking as peers, are thus members of the House of Lords. However, there's not much political influence in the House of Lords. It must be noted that as Dean Inge remarked, in general "the Church is absolutely free to make its own rules, without consulting . . . the law of the land. The only authority which it is bound to obey is the law of Christ, and what this is," the Dean gloomily added, "is by no means clear." Certainly it's clear that with such gentle uncertainties, the Dean could never become an Archbishop of Canterbury.

As for the Throne, as a constitutional function it now proceeds in the person of the new King, almost—not quite—as if no other king, laying aside his own crown, had ever shaken either. The generic modern popularity of the English Royal Family (which would certainly surprise some of the former members if they could come back) clearly had two periods and causes—the last years of Queen Victoria and of King George V, and their respectable bourgeois lives. Both knew earlier years of unpopularity—hers so manifested that she shrilly threatened to abdicate; his as a young monarch so ignored that his subjects sometimes failed to raise their hats when he drove through the London streets. It was King George V's final success that set the bourgeois-monarch pattern which his second son now earnestly conforms to and which his first son honestly could not, so would not, follow. Monarchy being originally a matter of hereditary principle rather than of conventional conduct, there are many English of all classes who still mystically regard the Duke of Windsor as their true king. As if he had died young, others still cherish him as the perfect Prince of Wales, which he was. But because their love has roots in his past, these adorers strangely want to know little of his present, which is so different. In the events of the past seven months the English have proved themselves moralistic rather than sporting-minded. Whatever fair play may mean on the green game fields, England still sternly expects every man to do his duty, especially if he is England's king, and can be harsh if he is on the losing side. That there is emotion in America about the Duke's no longer being on the throne from which certain American newspapers earlier bragged that they had removed him is fortunately largely unknown here. All that England knows is that she has utterly recovered from a painful family upset and wishes the neighbors would stop talking. Unfortunately, the upset has made English history, to which the English ordinarily give not silence but scholarly volumes. To millions of the rest of us, intently watching changing formulas in a shifting world today, what recently happened to the great British Empire, and above all what has not happened since, is still of interest.

JULY 14

Since apparently nothing in world affairs is a question of mere right and wrong any more, but rather a question of petroleum, manganese, or any of those vital things one nation has and another nation wants, it isn't surprising to learn here that what everybody (except the Spaniards, maybe) has been fighting for in Spain is not a principle but steel. While it was supposed that the Nazis were struggling to save Bilbao from Basque Bolshevism, what they've actually been killing for, it seems, is Bilbao's mines. With these fallen into General Franco's hands, they're as good as in Herr Hitler's pocket. This is a sharp loss to England. Aside from General O'Duffy's Irish brigade, now returned to Dublin from the Fascist Iberian front, the British have done no fighting—except in Mr. Eden's office. But for England's new, staggering Defence Program (also supposedly a pacific move) so much steel is needed that one-fifth of the ore was to have been imported from Bilbao. Armament has upped English steel needs from one million to a million and a half tons a month. The shortage is already being felt in peaceable automobile plants at Birmingham, where whole departments are on enforced half-time. Soviet orders amounting to £10,000,000 have just been refused. Bilbao is affecting people who never heard of it before.

Bilbao also brought thousands of people of twenty-one nationalities (and kroner, rubles, lire, belgas, francs, dollars, and pound notes) to a meeting held at Albert Hall to aid the Basque refugee children. Picasso and Heinrich Mann were supposed to appear but were nowhere to be seen. The Duchess of Atholl was supposed to talk, but, owing to microphone difficulties, couldn't be heard. Everyone heard Paul Robeson's songs. When he found he couldn't broadcast them from Moscow, he hurried all the way from Russia to sing them. Though England as a whole is still more in the mood of Gladstone than of Roosevelt or Blum, in all classes sympathy has been preponderantly for the Spanish government and against Franco. On the other hand, while the English are not for Franco's ally, Hitler, their growing pro-German sentiment is astounding. At the war veterans' recent Hyde Park parade, their outspoken dislike for their old French allies and their love for their old German enemies made one feel that no matter how a war turns out, it turns out wrong.

93

"London loves ballets . . ."

Irina Baronova in *Le Mariage d'Aurore*.

Alexandra Danilova and Leonide Massine
in *Gaité Parisienne*.

Leonide Massine and Tatiana Riabouchinska in *Scuolo di Ballo*.

The London ballet season, which began last autumn, has just started its summer lease on life. London loves ballets, and for four years now has replaced Paris as Terpsichore's home town. Five rival ballet troupes have contributed to the balletomane's recent satisfactions. Of the three visiting

groups, Miss Littlefield's Philadelphia Ballet, at the Hippodrome, has, even technically, delighted with its *Barn Dance*, a form of entertainment accepted here as America's national pastime. At the Coliseum, the Blum Monte Carlo Ballet, with Fokine as choreographer, has distinctly been rated as secondary to the other Russian troupe, principally owing to shaky male legs and ugly costumes. At Covent Garden, the de Basil Ballets Russes opened as, and still are, a triumph. Even at the old Châtelet in Paris, when Diaghilev was alive, we never saw a first night at which both spectators and dancers were more brilliantly ebullient; at which floral tributes were more florid (the Covent Garden Market's flower sheds next door do a flourishing ballet business); and at which a pandemonium of applause seemed more suitable. As the years pass since Diaghilev died, the early balletomanes age, but Massine in *Le Beau Danube* remains as young as he then was. He has matured only in unique grace. His choreography for *Symphonie Fantastique*, a feature of the Garden's second night (and unknown in Paris), in its use of plastic groups reminded visiting Parisians of *Les Noces* of the great old days. For the London performance, a pale and priceless new Bérard church set replaces the original black fifth-movement backdrop which made visibility impossible. The *première* ballerinas for the de Basil season are Riabouchinska, flawless in the *pas de deux* of *Cimarosiana*; Danilova at her perfect best in the cancan of *La Boutique Fantasque*; and always a little less fleet, Baronova, beautiful and technical in *Le Mariage d'Aurore*. At Covent Garden, you may smoke during the ballets, and between acts eat strawberries and cream at the bar. As the long summer season drags on, top hats disappear, ballet love becomes intense, and balletomanes sit sweating in flannels.

In Diaghilev's day, about 8 per cent of his dancing girls were English; Pavlova said she used English girls largely because they could develop technique without temperament. The English ballets normally operating in London prove this in a way; they are often excellent, but not contagious. At the King's Theatre in Hammersmith, the English Miss Marks, billed as Markova, with Dolin (Pat Kay, an Irishman), and Nijinska as choreographer, lead as the best of the local products. What used to be the Sadler's Wells ballet, which Constant Lambert devotedly worked for, is now called the Vic-Wells Ballet, with not very lush choreography by Frederick Ashton, who in turn sprang from Miss Rambert's Ballet Club. At the de Basil Ballets' first night, Lady Oxford (Margot Asquith) sat in a box; the second night, in a government omnibus box sat visiting Arabian sheiks in native dress, politely puzzled by the pirouettes but bravely toasting the British Empire in lemonade.

Now that it's safely over, the *News Chronicle* has inquired, "What's Wrong With Covent Garden Opera?" One thing wrong could be the *News Chronicle*'s and the *Manchester Guardian*'s critics' being refused their critics' tickets "on the instructions of Sir Thomas Beecham," whose conducting they, like everybody else, adversely criticized. We're willing to pay cash for future tickets, and add that Sir Thomas drowned even the voice of Flagstad, as Isolde; that *Prince Igor* was played practically backward, for scenes on end; that though English brasses are never good, for badness the Beecham brasses took the cake; that from the fourth row, ill-fitting scenery gave a full view of the stage's flies; that the production was poor, and the costumes sometimes laughable. Goossens' new Covent Garden

Readying the House of Commons for the opening of Parliament.

operatic novelty, *Don Juan de Mañara*, also discouraged critics with its intellectual evasion of tunes. The libretto was written by Arnold Bennett and was sung in English. The strangest moment was when a fatally poisoned Donna sang, "There is no antidote." The greatest musicianship of the season was in the opening of the Toscanini concerts, when the maestro, as if demonstrating his art in capsule, conducted "God Save the King."

OCTOBER 27

Engand is a reliable island. You can leave it for months, sure that on your return nothing, not even its latest news, will have changed. The subject may have altered, but the predication remains the same. Thus, whatever Europe's winter novelties may tragically turn out to be, English autumnal announcements feature the following comforting pattern: The King and Queen will have a rehearsal of their first State opening of Parliament, before opening it. The King and Queen still have to take a lift from their bedrooms in Buckingham Palace to their private bathrooms on the next floor. On an

97

official visit, the Duke of Kent tested a fresh-egg tester at the North London Exhibition, where a talking robot truthfully told His Royal Highness that he had no waistcoat on. There's a snooker-pool handicap tournament at the famous Thurston's, and sharks have been seen in the Thames. Colchester, illustrious for its bivalves, has served an oyster feast, with a toast to "the Armed Forces of the Crown." In addition to their toppers and jackets, Eton boys are now to have gas masks. The National Joint Committee for Spanish Relief has refused to be relieved of the Basque refugee children, whose six hundred Bilbao parents want them to come home. Mr. Anthony Eden has given the Continent what Downing Street calls another Plain Warning. The lapidated Sir Oswald Mosley has been given something similar by his doctors, who forbade him to speak for six weeks. British troubles in Palestine have been headlined by the *Times* as "The Nazareth Murders" and "Jerusalem Under Curfew." And the new London theatrical season rejoices in a play called *A Spot of Bother*.

Neither in their disparities nor in their conclusions can these items be regarded as unhappily special. Indeed, they have the good fortune to represent an ordinary day's news in a land which, on just such insularity, built a distant Empire—a land which, of all Europe, is sitting solidest today.

The annual London Stamp Exhibition at Dorland Hall was a proof. The entries were five times as numerous as last year, and ten times as valuable, totaling £150,000. The bewildering possession of three Kings in one year was unquestionably responsible for England's present stamp fever, which began as patriotism and ended in philately. The George V Silver Jubilee stamps, constituting a magnificently engraved series issued at £5 and now quoted around £20, first caught the loyal public eye, which was next focussed on the short-lived modernist photo-portrait stamps of Edward VIII and finally on the old-fashioned George VI Coronation issue. The Jubilee series' pictorial appeal—Australia's splendid King-on-a-Horse stamp, engraved after a snapshot taken by the *Daily Mirror,* and Canada's stamp of the King's yacht, *Britannia,* which was later scuttled—won popular response. Also, the Jubilee series' printing freaks, thanks to which profit could be made on engravers' errors, proved even more attractive. A plate flaw in the vignette of Windsor Castle which gave that pile two flagstaffs instead of one boosted the Gambia three-hapenny Extra Flagstaff variety, in blue and scarlet, to sixty shillings, and the rarer Hong Kong five-cent green and indigo to £20. South African stamps with four headplate flaws, which gave King George what collectors call (1) the Cleft Skull, (2) the Gash Behind the Ear, (3) the Gash in Front of the Ear, and (4) Dots at Top of Head and Base of Neck, now fetch £8 10s. for a set in blocks of four. Canada supplied a faulty one-cent of Princess Elizabeth that gives her a tear under the right eye. A Weeping Princess now fetches £10.

Stamps may mean madness to collectors or mere revenue to government, but to the rest of us, Dorland Hall exhibited, in multi-colored miniature, the hopes, regrets, labors, past histories, and current events which men, in

Anthony Eden was given an almost tender political loyalty by the British female public, who found him a handsome as well as an admirable statesman.

big lands or little archipelagoes, now live by. What caught our eyes were pictorials like Ecuador's gold-washers and sombrero-makers at work; Czechoslovakia's gray Second Mourning stamp for its late leader, Masaryk; China's new Chiang Kai-shek issue, with the timely, tragic words, "To Commemorate Unification;" the United States of America's apropos Constitution Commemorative; Spain's painful Viva Franco, Destruction of Toledo, and Burgos Anniversary; France's Unemployed Relief, and Tercentenary of Descartes (with the name of his *Discourse on Method* misquoted). The dictator stamps attracted crowds about the semiprofile of Hitler; the thirty-kopeck profile of Stalin with, behind him, the white ghost of Lenin, and behind both, the red flames of Revolution; and the Equestrian Statue of Mussolini issue, which had to be equestrian because he refuses to lend his face to a stamp. Italy's new Bimillennium of Augustus Caesar postage, the quaintest curio of the philatelists' show, featured stamps equipped with useful quotations from the Duce of antiquity, plus tags from Horace and Vergil. A ten-centesimo gray-green, picturing the bow of a trireme, quotes *"Mare pacavi* [I pacified the sea]"; a vermilion, with date palms, announces, "At my command and by my authority armies were led into Ethiopia"; and an expensive blue quotes Vergil: "As people to hold by every right both sea and land," and to prove it, bears the map of the Empire of Rome, extending from the Atlantic to the Euphrates, from the Rhine to North Africa. Vergil was a good poet in his time, but he makes a poor prophetic sibyl today.

Because people were worried about war, the stock exchanges have reacted so that now people are worried about both war and the stock exchanges. Everyone in Europe is convinced that he wants peace but the other fellow wants war—everyone, that is, except the Spaniards, who know they want war and wish a couple of the other fellows would stick to peace. Certainly diplomatists, who for generations have been considered as gentlemen occupied in getting their countries into war, have been busy saying anything they could think of which would keep peace. Ambassador von Ribbentrop was so busy keeping peace that he flew to Berlin on the eve of London's Non-Intervention meeting and so missed that session entirely. Whether it's true or not, there's a feeling in England, and, the English hope, in other places, that England holds the balance of power, which she will hold onto even if she has to fight for it, and which, if she lost, everyone else would start fighting for, and would not be able to hold anyway.

NOVEMBER 17

Though he was their former King, and only the United States of America's expected guest, the English and their press took the Duke of Windsor's annulled transatlantic visit more calmly than Americans. Indeed, the London *Times* took it so calmly that it grudgingly gave only a few inches to the Saturday cancelation announcement, and the equally anti-Edwardian *Telegraph* pointedly featured "Highlanders Killed By Arabs" as the day's big Empire news. Lord Beaverbrook's morning *Express* and *Evening Standard*,

A London landscape, with the Royal Exchange in the background.

which, if supposedly the Duke's best friends, are certainly his severest critics, editorially counseled him to live up to his farewell speech—"I now quit altogether public affairs"—and in a Low cartoon of a terrier hunting a rodent advised loyal Edwardians that it was Rat Week once more in London. The Leftist *Star* displayed a Workers' Travel Association official's interview with the Duke which stated, "The one certain bulwark against the Duke of Windsor becoming or desiring to become a dictator is his smile." And the sober Labour *Reynolds News*, in extenuation of his Bedaux guidance and Nazi housing survey, more sensibly pointed out that the Duke knows, "in fact, practically nothing of politics."

A valued part of the Royal Family's iconographic stability lies precisely in its members' being, unlike other people, devoid of current opinion. On this point the Constitution, public approval, and consequently the education of princelings is strict. English royalties' duty is toward an impersonal, peripatetic curiosity from which, even after years of experience, they are supposed to draw no conclusions. Thus when Queen Victoria holidayed in France, no one thought for a minute it was because she was pro-French. Equally, the Duke's visit to Germany was no more deemed to make him out pro-German than visiting the States could have made him pro-American, especially since (considering how different they are) he could not be pro-both.

England is still a place where, if partisanship is forbidden kings, it also is not forced on any lesser man. For private individuals, intolerance and having, at the risk of the affections, to take intellectual sides in everything aren't yet the fashion here. England is agreeably *démodée*.

Europe must indeed be moribund, since the three most discussed musical items of the past months have been three requiems—Verdi's at Salzburg, Brahms' and Fauré's at Queen's Hall. Mlle. Nadia Boulanger of Paris proved a unique *maestra* in directing the lofty, lyric Fauré, which the British called chill; fourteen thousand adorers failed to obtain seats for Toscanini's warmer Brahms, Toscanini's artistry now being at such a righteous pitch of popularity that if he directed "Three Blind Mice" it would draw (and probably sound) like Haydn. Queen's Hall has been finally redecorated, with its elderly verdigris charm and discomfort altered to cream paint, excellent seats of the wrong red, circular pink overhead lighting that looks like a jelly roll, and air-conditioning that efficiently substitutes for the natural old draughts.

The rarest London music was the bell-ringing in the towers of Saint Clement Danes, Saint Mary-le-Bow, and other City churches celebrating the tercentenary gathering of the Ancient Society of College Youths, who aren't young or collegiate, being mostly ripe country chaps who are the finest campanologists, or bell-pullers, left on earth or in the air. English campanologists have to be expert (the writhing bell rope may hang a man), strong (the great seventeenth-century bells weigh three tons each), and musical mathematicians, since the bells are rolled skyward in a series of strict and celestial musical changes. A long peal of 21,363 changes was once rung at Saint Lawrence's, Appleton, and took twelve hours. For the bell-ringers' evensong service held to honor the fraternity at Saint Paul's Cathedral, three courses of Stedman Cinques were first rung from the tower, while the pigeons fled in fright from the giant sound and in the plane trees below the starlings set up a contrapuntal twittering. During the service, in the Jesu Chapel behind the high altar one course of Stedman Triples was played on hand bells. They sounded like musical multiplication tables.

The rare, pleasant autumn—which some English fruit trees mistook for spring, and so bloomed again in celebration—has opened the annual November fox-hunting in a bad way, with slippery grass and too much pretty foliage for safe jumping. However, in Scotland, where bad weather knows its duty, deer-stalking is going into its third and best month. Deer-stalking was introduced from Germany by Victoria's Consort, but is popular with the English, being practiced almost exclusively in Scotland. Two rifles, stalking twice a week in the stiffest, fairest sport known here, need ten thousand acres of so-called deer forests, often without trees. Patience, hardiness, and marksmanship are required to shoot a wary stag at a hundred yards at dusk, after a day of silent, upwind stalking and sliding down Scotch screes so rocky that only trousers, not kilts, decently protect the descent. A party for two rifles would include also two stalkers to carry the weapons (.240s or .275s, with dumdum bullets), two flasks of whisky, and a pony boy, usually an old man who speaks nothing but Gaelic and who, when signaled by a lighted fire, brings up the pony and sledge on which the stag is finally dragged off, after a stalker has gralloched, or disemboweled, him. Hinds—the elderly ones are called yeods and are the sportsman's bane, since the old girls always give the alarm—are shot, and then not for sport, only in midwinter, when they must be thinned from the herd along with the extra switches, or stags with no points on their antlers. Stags aren't shot till their velvet is off, around October, in the rutting season. They are chosen for their points (a royal has twelve to his antlers), for their spread, and for their weight, which at three years is about fifteen stone, or two hundred and ten pounds. Of late, hikers have harmed stalking. It seems that one hiker can scare a stag to the other end of his ten thousand acres. Stags and hinds are red deer; does and bucks are fallow deer; and the roe deer, which are the best to eat, the English don't bother to make a sport of. In Scotland, stags are never stalked on the Sabbath.

Ten years ago, in his last performance at the Saint James's Theatre, Sir Johnston Forbes-Robertson presented, in the cast of *Twelfth Night*, himself, his friends, and members of his talented family to the number of fourteen. "His voice that rang the imagination like a bell," "his use of his arms in rhetoric," "his severe beauty," "the brow still unbesieged" made "of this infinitely graced actor" "the noblest Hamlet of them all." Such chance obituary phrases can make, connected, his fitting epitaph.

November 24

The King and Queen's appearance at the Palladium Music Hall's charity Royal Command performance made it the biggest vaudeville night in the year not only for those who attended but also for those who didn't. As usual, ten million radio listeners sat at home hearing the show broadcast and movies all over the island suffered the usual £100,000 slump, which is their annual sacrifice to the stage. Two years ago, movie men bought up the rights to the broadcast and suppressed it; this year they decided it was cheaper to listen in, like everybody else. These Royal Command performances can make a new performer and remake an old one; the bill is the pick of the top of the tree and the performance the peak of the vaudeville artist's career. The English music hall is a unique survival; it combines the exalted-star ritual of the Keith and Pantages days with the comforting low laughter of the old American burlesque. The Palladium's prize act this season featured the male Crazy Gang, impersonating the elderly female flower-sellers around the Eros statue in Piccadilly Circus. An English music hall is no place to take your aunt, unless she's English.

In each new reign, the incoming Court's standard—whether stiff or sociable—is a matter of interest to theatre managers in general. At the Command show, the performers claimed they didn't pull their punches—much. In their beflowered box, Their Majesties and the Duke and Duchess of Kent laughed as loudly as anybody, the royal brothers smoked cigarettes, the royal ladies helped themselves to chocolates, and all four joined Gracie Fields in singing the chorus of "Sally."

It's proof of the high degree of literacy sporadic on both the New York and London stages today that dramas in verse are now offered by commercial producers in their right minds. The importance of fine poetry in the theatre has just been demonstrated here at the Saint James's by Mr. Gilbert Miller's production of *The Silent Knight*, rewritten from the Hungarian by the English poet Humbert Wolfe. It is his poetry, more than the quaint fifteenth-century Italianate plot notion, that makes the play—his lovely, choice verbs and nouns, his varied vocabulary, and his rhymes, some as graceful and dry as Pope, some as funny and spotty as *The Ingoldsby Legends*. Even if we could read Hungarian, we'd expect only to find proof that Mr. Wolfe had borrowed nothing from the Danube. Like the unbeatable seventeenth-century English translators before him, his fitness lies in his being only original. *The Silent Knight*'s plot concerns a lovesick Hungarian warrior who, after his lady's first kiss, vows to be dumb for a period of three years—later reduced to eighteen months, though sometimes still feeling like three years, owing to monotonous scenery and medieval singing that retard the speedy finale, a dialogue with an executioner and a wedding on a revolving stage. Admirers of Miss Diana Wynyard feel that this new leading role of cruel coquette is not her style. To give the play its morbid, romantic fillip, a long-familiar pair like the New York Lunts or the Paris Tessier-Jouvet team would probably be the proper caper.

The extraordinary popularity of Damon Runyon's Broadway-jungle short stories, now appearing in the *Evening Standard*, has annoyed certain of the English more than somewhat. Readers, pro and con, have become writers to the editor to express their violent views. One correspondent, who signed himself Schoolboy, proclaimed, "I appreciate the sentiments of those whose reverence for the English Tongue has been outraged." A Mrs. Scratchley wrote in to say she couldn't imagine how cultured people can read "such coarse, common, revolting rubbish" and is sure that people in Washington

". . . the elderly female flower-sellers around the Eros statue in Piccadilly Circus."

and Boston don't. A Mrs. Moggridge of Wellington Square stated she was filled with "nausea, repulsion, and irritation." On the other hand, a Mr. Smith of South Norwood thinks Runyon's "claim to literary eminence is the beauty of his style;" other, more temperate gentlemen have called the knocks "classical baloney," recalled that Dickens was slanged for his cockney works, and asked how about a big hello for humor that is international. To encourage internationalists, the *Evening Standard* has opened a competition for the best original short stories written in Runyonese, with, as the announcement states, prizes of from "twenty-five potatoes" on down. However, in an effort to placate the readers who find Runyon "un-English, revoltingly transatlantic, and like an unpleasant noise," the paper has just printed a true-blue English author's story that contains the line "Get a bit of a belch off your stomach, like." Now, there's a pleasant noise.

Punch may be the ancestor of them both, but Eustace Tilley of *The New Yorker* is at least an uncle of Slingsby of *Night and Day*, the English weekly which for some months now has been tending to the Manhattanization of London. The title, *Night and Day*, was suggested by a garage sign that said "Day and Night"; while the magazine was still in the unnamed, dummy stage, an anonymous well-wisher kept telegraphing to advise calling it *Piccadilly*, and hasn't telegraphed since; the magazine sells best in London, Scotland, New York, and the Riviera, and never in Dublin. The weekly not only has been a surprise to bohemian intellectual and county-society readers, who either call it a Tory back-scratcher or else plain rude; it has also been a surprise to its editors, who thought that in England finding good writing would be as easy as finding bad drawings. The opposite has been the case. Only about 4 per cent of the manuscripts sent in are accepted, the 4 per cent coming principally, and secretly, from staid writers on the *Times*, glad of a chance to relax. Slingsby, who does *Night and Day*'s "Minutes of the Week" (equivalent to *The New Yorker*'s "Talk of the Town"), is really the travel-book best-seller, Peter Fleming—which nobody is supposed to know and several seem to. The coeditors, both Oxford men, are John Marks, translator of Céline, and Graham Greene, who, as the magazine's cinema critic, so thoroughly criticized Miss Shirley Temple that she's now suing him, the magazine, the publishers, the printer, and the distributor for libel, libel being a comprehensive affair in England. Evelyn Waugh does book reviews, Elizabeth Bowen the theatre. The publishers are Chatto & Windus, who, when publishers of Mark Twain, had a special room for him in their old office. The most special use he ever put the room to was to say in it, "The reports of my death have been greatly exaggerated."

DECEMBER 1

Parliament and the Church Assembly have, in their separate ways, each been debating grave, combustive questions. Parliament's problem concerns coal, via a bill for compulsory amalgamation of colliery undertakings that will affect pitmen, owners, and public alike, but not in like ways. Already it's clear that the nobler the owners, the nobler their resignation. It's noticeable here that, in the twentieth century, individuals privileged since the seventeenth show, perhaps because they've had so much for so long, a greater philosophy in the face of the changing times than do the nineteenth-century Victorian parvenus. The brave Tudor spirit, both as to riches and reflection, still slightly obtains. The Church's combustive problem deals only with a sort of up-to-date fragment of hell-fire—divorce. On January 1 comes into effect humorist A. P. Herbert's Matrimonial Causes Act, whose only gaiety lies in making divorce easier. In preparation for the new year, the Archbishop of Canterbury and churchmen have declared the Church remarriage of innocent as well as guilty divorcés to be "scandalously inappropriate" to the service lines "till death us do part," and pronounced against "eccentric clergymen" who marry remarriers. The Assembly's Lord Cecil has even proposed compiling a Parliamentary measure to forbid all churchmen to perform the ceremony for a person "whose spouse by a former marriage" still lives—a measure which, if retroactively considered, would criticize the blessed connubial relations of many members of Parliament, of the House of Lords, and of cockney society besides. That Parliament would, as even the Church fears, rebuff the Church's measure clarifies the Church's curious position—that of asking the State to legalize State-Church doctrines which, however appropriate canonically, differ from the State's laic laws. Bold minds consider that only by the disestablishment of the Established Church could the Church free itself, not only for the full scope of its Pauline principles, but also for a true tentmaker's revival.

The best thing about the English theatre is the English critics. What they write against a play is unfortunately usually better than what the author wrote for it, and breakfast with a review is apt to be funnier than supper after the first night of a show. London is the reverse of Paris, where, if the *critique* is childish, the dominant half-dozen playwrighting minds are mature. London is also unlike Paris in that the semi-institutional Old Vic, though devoted to national classics, like France's Comédie-Française, manages to be the best and liveliest theatre in the land. Old Vic's *Richard III*, starring the admirable Emlyn Williams, offered a notable example of the fine cheap costumes, sensitive skeleton sets, robust acting, dash, devoted intelligence, and inexpensive seats which should be found in all State theatres and usually aren't. "The man Shakespeare," as Queen Elizabeth once privately called him, is again the most popular playwright in town. *Macbeth* has followed *Richard III*, which followed Gielgud's *Richard II*, and even *Cymbeline* has been revived, with a new last act written in by the Irishman George Bernard Shaw. We regret to announce that Covent Garden's ice ballet has, however, melted from sight. This remarkable spectacle, sponsored by Mr. Bruce Ottley, renowned balletomane, featured Olympic skaters careening around as Hindu houris in a palmy, southern opus called *The Brahman's Daughter*. Skating stomach dancers, skating sweetmeat sellers, a skating parasol-bearer, and a Tommy Atkins hero, skating toward love in a sun helmet, were sights such as, in all our travels, our wondering eyes had never met before.

People who believe in signs and portents have plenty of reading matter here. The anguished financial pages' prognostications as to what Wall Street and the City will do next are accompanied in most newspapers by horoscope columns which, in case readers have lost faith in their brokers, should restore their belief in the stars. Thus the *Sunday Chronicle*'s horoscoper, Gipsy Petulengro (his address is Pump Yard, Manchester), declares that "those who derive their income from investments should have a good period at the beginning of the New Year," though, for those born under the Sign of the Cancer, "some business setbacks are likely." The *Referee*'s Anita da Silva, who also concentrates on people worried more by margins than by broken hearts, furnishes the romantic touch to "a decided improvement may be looked for" by adding, "The lucky color is sky blue." The *Express*, whose policy is blunt accuracy about everything, has a horoscoper unafraid to state, "This week's good days for buying are Monday, Friday; for selling, Thursday, Saturday. Money is to be made in real estate, minerals." For the merely superstitious he adds that they'd better wear a sapphire to make sure. At most London corner stationers, the one-shilling *American Astrology Magazine* sells neck and neck with the sixpenny British *Prediction*; in select Mayfair, each sells more than the rational *New Statesman*.

People here are not only worried about money. They are also weary of realities which brains don't seem to solve and from which stargazing and a recall to religion—both definitely and recently on the increase—are probably the symptomatic refuges, where man, as often before, can sit his troubles out. In the meantime, active realists are placing more hope for relief in the new British Commonwealth-American trade pacts, since they will loosen transatlantic money, if any is left, and anyhow tighten transatlantic democratic bonds. For in Europe right now, everything comes down to two things—cash and credo. This year closes with trade treaties between nations of similar political notions being regarded as optimistically as those medieval royal-cousin intermarriages once calculated to keep the peace, with, today, a *dot* of busy freight boats substituting for the bride's provinces or pearls. Indeed, the whole setup of Europe now seems tragically *passé*—a kind of Dark Ages three-cornered crusade of Christian democrats against paynim Fascists, Nazis, and Communists, but without Jerusalem as the goal. For of course England already has Jerusalem. As a matter of fact, nobody seems to know what the goal is. It's probably something which is also not new—just the terrible old financial and physical survival of the fittest.

DECEMBER 8

A list of nonfiction best-sellers just published here by the *Observer* contains some surprises for Americans. One of the favorites is the Americanized format of England's King James' version of the Bible, which sold twenty-five thousand copies on its first day, an all-century high for what is, after all, not the new book of the year. Another favorite is *The New Yorker Album*. *Gone With the Wind*, Wilkins' *And So—Victoria*, Harley Street Cronin's *The Citadel*, and Pilgrim's *So Great a Man* are the fiction best-sellers here, as they are in America. The Christmas sellout for juvenile bookworms in this country is their parents' choice—the American tale of Ferdinand, the popular pacifist Spanish bull.

The most-discussed English books to be republished in America are Huxley's decisive *Ends and Means*; Roberts' *The House That Hitler Built*, of special interest if Lord Halifax's recent structure turns out to be only a house of visiting cards; and Joan Grant's *Winged Pharaoh*. This volume features the author's belief that she is the reincarnation of the First Dynasty Princess Sekhet-a-ra, whose life (as her own life) Mrs. Grant relates. Indubitably the most permanent of the English literary exportations is, as its author, Harold Nicolson, terms it, the newly invented "indirect biography" entitled *Helen's Tower*. It's part of what will be a series called In Search of the Past. In portraying the fine figure of his vice-regal uncle, Lord Dufferin, Nicolson adds his own profile, as a noticing and noticeable nephew. And as a descendant of the noble and acquisitive Clandeboye family, castigated by Sir Walter Scott in *Rokeby*; as a former diplomat; as the scholarly, fecund book editor of the *Telegraph*; as, even, the husband of V. Sackville-West (author of *Pepita*), Mr. Nicolson somehow combines—though without necessarily mentioning them—all his private legacies and public participations, focusing them on one of his family's and his country's important figures. *Helen's Tower* demonstrates again the success of that special formula by which English biography, in its richness and its generality, almost invariably excels the personal record in other tongues.

One of the most curious English books, which apparently will not be exported, is Miss Edith Sitwell's *I Live Under a Black Sun*. This is a poetic, visually written volume—a book with loveliness and life floating in it, like upside-down reflections in a long river, on which the boatman's eyes, fascinated, gaze. The book deals with the anguished existence of the author of *Gulliver's Travels* and his Stella and Vanessa, all brought forward to modern times, but so gently that the transformation of Jonathan Swift into Jonathan Hare and the modernization of the ladies and the wars bring no shock or even disturbing reality.

The London Gallery has given the city its second exhibition of surrealism. A flatiron studded with nails, a glass eye in a birdcage, a bracelet of false teeth were leaders in this year's list, presented as Objects—Interpreted, Oneiric, Perturbed, Found, Invented by a Schizophrenic Lunatic, etc. The objects by Dali, Miró, Eluard, Breton, and others were declared to be not art and at first were refused entry by the British customs officers. What the British customs probably needs is a few Douanier Rousseaus.

The King recently visited Launceston Castle in Cornwall, where he received, as first visiting monarch since Charles I, certain feudal dues from those who enjoy ancient Duchy tenures of the land. In lieu of rents, the King, by custom, was presented by the mayor with a pound of pepper and a hundred shillings; Lord Clifden and Mrs. Rolt, between them, gave one gray cloak for the Manors of Pengelly and Cabilla; for the Manors of Lanihorne, Elerky, Battens, and Penvose he received a brace of greyhounds, a pair of gilt spurs, and a pound of cummin. One gentleman had to offer a salmon spear and a load of wood; the Mayor of Truro had to give a bow d'arburne. It's good that most of us here are permitted to pay our landlords in cold cash. Though often too hard to find, it's easier to raise, even on the last day of the month, than whippets or caraway seed.

Horcher of Lutherstrasse is now also Horcher of Old Burlington Street. Like the Berlin restaurant, the new London branch is for gourmets only. It's costly, is the most recherché rendezvous in town, and is lighted by candles in fine old silver candelabra. The *Krebschwänze* and venison are sent from Germany; the remarkable wines are brought from the Rhine, Pfalz, and the   109

Moselle; the cream, butter, and eggs are English, and the German chef is glad to have all he needs of them, for a change. Hedonists have grieved to see such great Parisian restaurants as Voisin, Montagné, and, recently, Foyot's economically close down. Berlin's Horcher and Paris's Larue are almost the only renowned old European *traiteurs* left, both having survived on their artistic indifference to French and German thrift.

The local unofficial estimates of England's and America's paper losses in the recent stock crash are £5,000,000,000; preliminary Christmas shopping is a spot lower than at any time since what was called the new prosperity in 1933; and the Conservatives are cheerfully preparing for the real slump of 1940, when the armament program should be complete, by planning a victorious General Election in 1939, while conditions are still in their favor, lest His Majesty's Loyal Opposition, the Labour Party, should perhaps plan to do the same thing in 1941.

Presenting the plum pudding, an Arthur Rackham illustration for Charles Dickens' *A Christmas Carol.*

O ne of the few December holiday rules still obtaining here is that the Christmas pudding should be ready by Saint Andrew's, the last day of November, and that all of the household who will partake of it, from master down to scullery maid, must have given the ingredients a stir for luck. Christmas-pudding recipes here today fall into three epochs—Georgian recipes, which feature beer, rum, and brandy as moisteners; Victorian, which go in for quantities of costly, un-Danish fresh eggs, sometimes grated potatoes as well as flour, and stout as a blackener; and modern. The modern, alas, tend to use fresh fruit juices for the sake of the children, in place of adult beverages. All three feature grated raw carrots and Demerara sugar as shrewd counterbalancers of too much candied orange peel.

England is the only country doing much about broadcasting television, which, no matter what anybody does about it, still looks as though it were in the stereopticon stage. The television Christmas Day program will offer a football match, an American cabaret, the gourmet Boulestin showing how to serve the Christmas wines (which for most folk will be brown ale from The Pig and Whistle), and a special pantomime. While West End holiday pantomimes, such as this year's *Beauty and the Beast,* have recently revived interest as money-makers, connoisseurs still deplore the aesthetic loss in their modernizing. Today they are like innocent, garish revues, with the panto or fairy-story part (once merely a kernel) now providing nearly the whole show, which was formerly a proper harlequinade, peopled by *commedia-dell'-arte* characters, such as Harlequin, Columbine, Pantaloon, maybe a local red-nosed policeman, and the like.

By extending drink licenses from the usual midnight closing to 2:00 a.m., London will heighten the holiday gaiety to be offered for Christmas and New Year's Eve by most of her eighteen major night haunts, only about ten of which Londoners speak kindly of. Smartest are the Ritz's frenchified *café chantant,* Ciro's, and the Four Hundred Club, most recherché of the bottle-party law-loopholers. In Soho, the London Casino is the butter-and-egg floor-show palace, topped in opulent style only by the Savoy; the Café de Paris has a cabaret. In Park Lane, the Dorchester and Grosvenor House specialize in a specifically British formula of American and English lovelies; Mayfair still holds onto the old Florida, first of the great "bottle clubs" (which Parliament may pounce down on soon). Near Oxford Circus, traditional scene of collegiate revelry, is the Paradise Club. The only noticeable Negro *boîte* is The Nest, with a mixture of Harlem blackbirds and West Indian high yellows. A resort few Londoners speak of at all is curiously called The Midnight, since it opens at 2:00 a.m. to serve near-beer to that certain section of Soho, male and female, busy earlier during the day and night on street corners, giving tips at dog or horse races, milling round the Blackfriars wrestling ring, or arranging things in boxing circles. Remarkable swing music, performed by casual customers, can be heard at The Midnight, provided a deafening fight doesn't break out first.

The Sunday theatre "clubs," another curious London evasion—in this case only of the censor, the Sunday closing law, and commercialized stage

Overleaf: London celebrates the New Year, Piccadilly Circus.

Two of Soho's famous continental restaurants: Restaurant de Paris and Gennaro's Rendezvous.

tastes—are also enjoying special holiday animation. To the long line of private clubs, such as the Gate and the Arts, which have in the past courageously produced shockers like Shaw and Strindberg, and more recently Odets and Housman's *Victoria Regina*, has been added the Group Theatre, specializing in plays by Auden, Spender, and the much-discussed Isherwood. It lately featured a rousing intelligentsia first night of MacNeice's *Out of the Picture*. The other novelty is the Unity, which has just installed its workers' theatre in a remade Noncomformist chapel. Unity is very Left, and among its actors features Paul Robeson, now determined to give up Hollywood and appear only in works which are "sociologically a sound statement of the conditions of the Negro in the capitalist scheme of things."

A report on the scheme of things one hundred and fifty years ago, taken from the yellowed files of the *Morning Post* of 1787, has just come to light. According to England's special-from-the-American-Revolution correspondent, "Mr. [George] Washington is said to be in a fair way of being made the American Dictator. If once invested with that authority, it is not impossible 'Chance may crown him.'" Despite the time and blood spent, apparently the times don't change much; titles—fear of them, respect for them—dominate the vocabulary still making the front pages of the world today. We're probably lucky that, among other permanent big figures, Santa Claus also hasn't altered.

The London Season is more precise than any that is arranged by nature. Spring here has been getting under way with snow in Yorkshire, but the calendrical city season burst into bloom regardless and, as is the custom on the first Monday in May, with the Royal Academy art exhibition at Burlington House in the morning and Covent Garden grand opera at night. During the ensuing three months, this season will launch twelve hundred debutantes at coming-out parties; will provide for the needs of next year's London needy through its fabulous charity balls; will include, by special decision of the King, four Courts for unmarried and two for married women; will feature Ascot, the Aldershot Tattoo, tennis tourneys on green lawns, military tournaments on wide plains; and will finally burst into a finish at the Goodwood races at the end of July. There can, if desired, be added a rather urban week of August yachting at Cowes. Then it will be the twelfth of the month, with the grouse waiting to be shot punctually on the northern moors. The new country season will have begun.

1938

"Of [London's] eighteen major night haunts . . . smartest are the Ritz's frenchified *café chantant,* Ciro's. . . ."

It's odd that the spring city season always has to be opened by an art exposition sponsored by a society in which art so clearly ended long ago. Indeed, thousands of English seem to be attending this year's Royal Academy show because they can be sure of not seeing Wyndham Lewis's portrait of T. S. Eliot, easily the most important modern-mannered artwork submitted to the hanging committee. It was rejected amidst epithets, cheers, jeers, and letters to the *Times*, and finally housed at the Leicester Galleries. Of the endless roomfuls of canvases which the Royal Academy accepted, few of the pictures are in the best sense academic, and those portraying the Coronation, the King, and both Queens certainly don't look royal. Except for the water colors, which have that private apologetic air that marks real talent here, the exhibition seems distinguished for the boldness of its mediocrity and air of hard labor. What has been termed the worst press in thirty years called the show positively unlively. Ninety-seven years ago, a newspaper said that Turner's Academy landscape looked like "nothing in nature except eggs and spinach." That's the kind of bad press and good painting which the RA seems, unfortunately, unable to attract nowadays.

Covent Garden's opening week produced some of the grandest opera Europe has heard in years. And some of the hardest luck. When Lotte Lehmann, as the Marschallin, had a chill and walked out on the opening act of the first *Rosenkavalier* performance, a leg came off fat Baron Ochs' sofa. Furthermore, an anachronistic wirehaired fox terrier stole the eighteenth-century levee scene, and the lady spy's hoopskirt flew waist-high after the Presentation of the Rose episode. In the second week, because of Tauber's illness Mozart's *Entführung* was at the last minute replaced by *Rosenkavalier*, which a bewildered gentleman next to us enjoyed all evening as Mozart, pronouncing it a great relief from that awful Strauss, whose *Elektra* he'd had to listen to the night before. However, from Covent Garden's comic muddles certain things became clear—for one, the fact that with the world in a military and monetary mess, music seems to be a greater public pleasure for Londoners than it was in the days when all were rich and peacefully carefree. It was also clear when Lehmann had her second go at the Marschallin, one of the peak performances of her career, that handsome Lemnitz as Octavian and high-toned little Berger as Sophia (both from the Berlin State Opera) made with her a trio that New York should hear—the finest known to *Rosenkavalier* connoisseurs since the Strauss piece was first produced.

Noël Coward's new opus *Operette*, is so fashionable that when the curtain rises, His Majesty's Theatre is half empty. Though the chic late diners finally fumble in, the theatre is not full even when the last curtain goes down. The piece got poisonous reviews. There are many solid reasons for disliking it—if the listener can think of anything solid while wafting through a nebulous ether of memory, remorse, "Florodora" pompadours, reality, delight, illusion, allusion, smiles, tears, and some songs (mostly remarkable for the lyrics). America's Peggy Wood sings with high, sweet, Anglican purity, the chorus girls have voices like thrushes, and the dowager Irene Vanbrugh

W. H. Auden, Christopher Isherwood, and Stephen Spender.

plays a five-minute scene written and acted with all the civilization gained during two talented lives—the actress's and the author's. Apparently not ten people out of a hundred like *Operette*. Our applause alone had the strength of ten the night we were there.

It's usually difficult on arriving in London, let alone on leaving it, to discover what the English are thinking. At the moment, anybody could come in and go out on the same day and know all. Clearly, England is divided (by what proportions only a general election would show) into people who either detest or admire Prime Minister Chamberlain; who think either that Eden could head a third party or that he is already justly headed for oblivion; who believe either that the League of Nations is still a coat of shining armor or that it's a stuffed shirt. Not for years have policies here been debated so personally; rarely has one seen the English of all classes thinking not as classes but in terms of emotion. The spirit, if not the doctrine, of His Majesty's Loyal Opposition has produced minority minds in people used to being in the majority. The air-armament scandal is going to be a bomb when it breaks. Classes in gases are being held with ladies learning how to adjust gas masks on bearded civilians, and beards are already counted more of a risk than smooth chins in the next war.

MAY 24

Apparently weekends were invented by the English so they could get away from London. Certainly the hegiras are approved by the government, since the House of Commons never meets on Saturday, thus leaving all members free to flee town Friday evening. As peers seem to do things more slowly, the House of Lords gets ready for its weekends, which last till Tuesday, by rising on Thursday at tea. The two extra days were originally needed for the coach-and-four drive to and from the ancestral country mansions which many lords, alas, have since lost; however, they still possess those two precious idle days. Weekending, as a powerful English institution, is more important than ever this year because of the recent un-English goings-on in Europe. As if to demonstrate their three great traditional talents—for playing politics, for accumulating wealth, and for designing lovely landscapes—the English work best at the first two against a background developed by the third. For generations most of what has happened to mortals and money in London, and often what has happened to Europe, has first been planned in the talk of prominent Englishmen weekending with a purpose among the green trees and fields of some beautiful bucolic shire. For the last few months the purpose and weekends have been intense. So important were the supposedly pro-German weekends at Cliveden that Cliveden's host, Lord Astor, wrote a letter to the *Times* in protest at being called a Fascist, leaving to his American-born politician wife the more ticklish job of writing a second denial to Labour's *Daily Herald*. The truculent weekends of pro-British Winston

Lotte Lehmann as the Marschallin in *Der Rosenkavalier*.

Churchill have nearly singlehanded weakened the Chamberlain government into reshuffling its Cabinet and retiring its heckled Air Minister. As the dissatisfaction over army enrollment, taxation, and foreign relations continues, worried weekending politicians land in private airplanes on Georgian estates' golf links, Hitler and Henlein are discussed in Adam drawing rooms, pilots and secretaries with last-minute dossiers are housed in the Queen Anne wing. Hostesses order what are officially called long dinners—lengthy repasts beginning with hothouse melon and supposedly ending in grave discussion—instead of jolly short dinners, which start with scandal and end with bridge. Hosts are bringing out their best *goût-anglais* brandies (less sweet than for the French) and producing their great ports. Male or female, Parliamentarian or private taxpayer, high up in big houses or low and loyal in cottages, the English are worried about their present state and future history. Everyone knows, including the Germans, what they're worrying about: Will the Germans really provoke war (or provoke others to provoke it), and if so, when, how, where? Will the English be ready, with whom, by what means, and for what? On such topics people could talk all night, as alarmed governing weekenders, awkwardly loaded with an easily attacked island, an empire, and the last bulwarks of European democracy, do indeed converse. Yet the simple situation can be put in a few awful words.

Or, as the Home Office prefers, the situation can be put in lots of words. According to a recent official announcement, the English can expect enemy bombers upon hearing, as an air-raid alarm, "a fluctuating or warbling signal of varying pitch in which the frequency is not less than 10 per cent above and below the mean pitch, the complete cycle of each fluctuation to extend over a period of two to five seconds."

It's noteworthy that English weather records have been officially kept only since 1815, the year of the Battle of Waterloo, when the French lost through being unexpectedly stuck in the rain and mud. Nevertheless, private documents exist to declare that 1938's drought is the worst since 1785. Potatoes are twice their proper price and salmon, through their inability to leap up the shallow streams to wed, are so scarce in their usual haunts that anglers figure each fish caught will cost around £65 all told, after lodge rent, riparian rights, etc., have been taken care of. Dried grass on the race courses, now in their money-making season, has made the entries of valuable horses rare. In Scotland, Saint Andrew's famous golf course has closed to save the greens. Certainly it's not often that nature punishes Heaven itself; this year's drought has dried church organs till they're off pitch. While parish ladies with teakettles and steam have swelled the little village pipes to normal, in the great Gothic cathedrals, as the mammoth organs peal forth, God is praised out of tune.

JUNE 1

When the German-Czechoslovakian news appeared in the morning papers, May 22 looked as though it would be a special European-crisis day. By

"... the unassuming brick residence ... of the Prime Minister ... England's dominant political brain ... at Number 10 Downing Street. ..."

121

noon in London it looked like any average quiet English Sunday. In the streets, unemployed veterans of the last war were selling the customary violets, not extra editions, for there were no extra editions to sell. In Hyde Park, of three soapbox orators, one, who was white and old, was sermonizing against Christianity; another, middle-aged and black, was discoursing on the British Union; the third, a blond stripling in a red sweater, was lecturing on socialism. Before the Prime Minister's house in Downing Street, where anxious crowds might have been expected, there was a knot of four portly out-of-town women, worrying as to where they should lunch. There were also two small boys with scooters, running races against each other. They had picked the quietest street in London to run them in.

Maybe modern European history is now being made by England's saying and doing nothing, for the first time since modern European history began. Certainly England's finally acting the strong and silent Englishman has upset all the Continental characters' calculations. Since noisy talk is so effective in some circles today, certain nations are wondering if England's being silent is necessarily any proof of England's being strong. If strength consists only in having on hand more military equipment than Germany, in being willing to go to war, and in being willing to start a war rather than wait to be warred on, then England is indeed weak. England, being a democracy, with all the precious inefficiency that comes from men's having enough liberty to make money, to make gardens, to make a million different odd things—even to make, if they choose, fools or rich rogues of themselves, rather than obediently making machines, military motions, and sacrifices—England, being, as we say, a democracy, is now in no position to compete suddenly with totalitarian competence. And as for war, England doesn't want either to start or to be dragged into one, which doesn't mean that England isn't trying to catch up with the rest of the world in armament or that England would not fight at some given point, now incalculable. The Monday after the Czechoslovakian crisis, fifty of the British army's best bombing planes flew over London, sixty fighting planes circled the suburbs; four hundred planes in all flew over the island in a so-called demonstration for Empire Air Day. For all Mr. Chamberlain's unintellectual, unidealistic, taciturn leadership, he so far has had the majority of the country with him because he is keeping it out of war. If he fails at that or something else and falls, his job, it is supposed, will then be offered to the Opposition Labour chief, Attlee, who, on being unable to compass a House majority, will willingly watch the premiership pass to youngish Anthony Eden. Eden's name did not appear in the papers in connection with the Sunday crisis. As a matter of fact, that day he was playing croquet in Kent. It is not yet his political turn; it is also probably not in his character to wish to embarrass his country's government into breaking down prematurely, even though he may yet have the task—and the later it comes, the harder it will be—of building up another government under similar conditions.

Everything that is happening in Europe now is happening according to the characters, rather than the politics, of a few leading men. What is taking place here is psychology, not history. History will come later.

Sybil Thorndike and Emlyn Williams in *The Corn is Green*.
The protean Emlyn Williams, both ornament and stimulant in the
British theatre, whose talents burst from him as canny playwright,
actor, and memorialist. As the murderous young charmer in his own
dramatic concoction *Night Must Fall*, the stage property he carried
about with him with sinister élan was a hatbox, a smart piece of
luggage which contained the head of a recent benefactress.

In the succeeding *The Corn Is Green*, the actor-playwright, ge-
nially autobiographical this time, lent us a page from his early life as
a Welsh laborer's son, educated out of his constricting environment
by an exceptional teacher (enacted by the awesome Sybil Thorndike).
No stranger to Shakespeare either, as attested by his acclaimed
Gloucester in the Old Vic's *Richard III* (page 14).

Tamara Geva and Raymond Massey in "Massey's lamentable
production of *Idiot's Delight*...."

John Gielgud offers a toast in *Dear Octopus*.

Alfred Lunt and Lynn Fontanne in *Amphitryon 38*. The greatest, most powerful, and most seductive of any theatrical marital couple. Their appeal to the eyes and ears of audiences was unique. A singularly unified pair whose teasing interplay on the stage was one of their major gifts of intimacy to us. Which of them was the more popular and in what role? These were questions which could never be answered in the overwhelming satisfactions they each gave, again and again and again, to us out front, eavesdropping and spying on the most gifted, remarkable display of domestic and professional felicity.

In the way of things to do, see, bet on, buy, listen to, participate in, travel far and near for, and spend money upon, there is more going on in England in one month than is advertised for the whole summer in any other country in Europe. Most of the events occur every year; some have taken place annually for centuries; in sum, they represent the accumulated momentum of the easy English existence. Among old customs, there's the planting of the penny hedge at Whitby, the midsummer bonfires in Cornwall, the swan-upping on the Thames. There are in rotation thirty-seven city and county horse, livestock, and flower shows, including the London cart-horse parade, which fills fashionable Regent's Park with proud coal-cart drivers and their handsome nags. There will be, besides bowls, archery tournaments, Wimbledon, and the Test Matches, more than a hundred important polo, yachting, rowing, and racing events. As for the dozens of rural music festivals, the most important opening has been the Glyndebourne Opera House's. The sunset on the Sussex hills and the parade of evening clothes on the lawn and in the garden were perhaps better than the evening of Verdi's *Macbeth* which followed. While the death waltz after the King's murder gives way to a sudden chorus as superb as parts of Verdi's *Requiem*, the *opus* is tum-tum, oompah, and so-so Verdi, an odd choice for a house hitherto devoted to Mozart. The lighting and scenery were so imaginative and inventive as to make Covent Garden's operatic effects seem like old chromos.

Augustus John's one-man exhibition showed his power to draw fashionable intellectuals to the Tooth Gallery as well as to portray them on canvas. It also showed, unfortunately, how poor his landscapes can be and how severe may be the judgment of age on one who in his youth was the leading bohemian of his generation. In the theatres, the two most popular pieces are Raymond Massey's lamentable production of *Idiot's Delight* at the Apollo and *Amphitryon 38*, with the Lunts, at the Lyric. Whatever critics have said these plays don't do, they succeed in making people laugh about war—while there's still time.

JUNE 21

O ne of the mistakes which everybody, including the English, makes about the English is the assumption that the English are unmusical. As near as we can figure out, the English are now openly—and have long been covertly—pushovers for music. Tunes certainly were always well thought of, for native royalty like Henry VIII and Mary Queen of Scots used to compose their own. It wasn't till the Hanoverian dynasty was imported from Germany—supposedly the home of harmony—that kings of England let music slide in favor of the less cultivated, squirarchal joys which even the squires deplored in a monarch. Today London is the only city in Europe where seats for Toscanini's concerts are so precious that music lovers draw for them in a sort of sweepstake, as if they were horses. Over a weekend the concert announcements and musical criticisms in the Saturday *Telegraph* and the Sunday *Times* and *Observer* are ampler than you'd see in any three French papers for a month of Sundays. No longer in Vienna could there suddenly spring up, as in London, a popular Schubert Society founded to produce Schubert's unpopular works. The founder of the Society is the distinguished lieder singer and Schubert authority Reinhold von Warlich, who was the first to sing the *Winterreise* in London as a song cycle, the way Schubert intended it to be sung. The Society's president is the composer's great-niece Miss Carola Geisler-Schubert, once a great friend of Brahms; its royal patroness is Princess Helena Victoria, who always shoulders the musical end of the Royal Family's duties; the Council includes Fritz Kreisler, the Earl of Plymouth, the Countess of Winchelsea and Nottingham, and other notables. Schubert left between eight and nine hundred songs, of which only about one hundred are ever sung here. The Society will give hearings to what's rarest among the other seven hundred duos, chorals, etc. The first concert honoring Schubert was to have been held at the Austrian Embassy. Austria having been suddenly deprived by the *Anschluss* of its Embassy, the music was played at the American Women's Club.

In reality the proof of England's innate musicality lies not among the grandee listeners but among the simple singers. English choirs are now esteemed as the best in Europe, for they have an impersonal, disciplined purity of tone and pitch which distinguishes them from the *Schwärmerei* and ragged individualism of German and French singing groups. In their recent revival, English singing societies have become as common over the island as larks, and often as humble and bucolic; they entice hamlet singers by the thousand to the bigger towns whenever competitions are held. Singing societies are often connected with the church, as in Canterbury Cathedral's and Tewkesbury Abbey's musical festivals; sometimes they are mixed with nationalism, as in Aberystwyth's three-day League of Youth Eisteddfod. They can be tied to the energetic apron strings of ladies' community clubs in any shire, are oftenest merely an organic English desire for dulcet part singing of catches, glees, carols, oratorios, Elizabethan roundelays, and the like. Among the noted provincial choirs, that of Leeds is the most famous. Glasgow's Orpheus is fine, as is Lewes's Musical Society. The London Oriana specializes in madrigals; the London Choral features symphonies; all are trained to tackle Handel's *Messiah*, Bach's B-Minor Mass (or *Saint Matthew Passion*), Elgar's *Dream of Gerontius*, Coleridge-Taylor's perennial *Hiawatha*, Purcell's *Fairy Queen*, and Walton's *Belshazzar's Feast*, easily the grandest choral work of our decade. Choirs here are superb because English singers are best not as professionals but as amateurs.

On the sidewalks of London, the daily sad, sweet hymn-singing of the still-unemployed Welsh miners is very pretty, too.

Three-quarters of all the English novels published are published to be rented, not bought. Ever since the days of the now-defunct Mudie's Select Lending Library, romance let out to bookworms at about tuppence a day has been the bane of the book trade. Now the publishers of unromantic books have something to worry about, too—the Penguin series, serious tomes which sell at sixpence each. The Penguin volumes are sold everywhere; even in slot machines, like chewing gum. Formerly the publishers of the Penguins specialized in reprints of detective stories and general favorites like Shakespeare, and paid the author (if alive) one farthing in royalties on each book. The new series consists of originals, not reprints. If published in the normal fashion, each book would cost the reader between $1.80 and $4.00, instead of the twelve and a half cents which is the regular Penguin price. The two latest have sold at the rate of twenty-five hundred copies a week, and if they didn't appeal only to intellectuals and Leftists, they would drive the other publishers nuts. Both concern current affairs. The first is *Mussolini's Roman Empire*, a thoughtful, angry, elaborately documented compilation of facts against Il Duce by G. T. Garratt, the Manchester *Guardian*'s war correspondent in Abyssinia and Spain. The second is *Searchlight on Spain*, by the Duchess of Atholl, Conservative Member of Parliament, until recently whip of the National Government, and now known as the Red Duchess. Her book is principally a continuation of her questions in the House of Commons to the Premier and her odd private correspondence with him demanding to know why he hasn't intervened against Franco in Spain. Both books attack British diplomacy, both add to that painful sense of partisanship which is one of the horrors of civil war, even among those not fighting in it.

JUNE 28

The European history being made right now is going to make queer reading someday. Indeed, it looks strange to some of us already. Germany has just refused to pay her Province of Austria's debts because, Germany declares, the Dawes loans were political, not private. Germany has also just demanded of the Rothschild family what looks like £2,000,000 ransom for the imprisoned non-Aryan Baron Louis de Rothschild. Germany considers the ransom compensation for the failure of the Baron's Viennese Credit Anstalt, a failure which the rest of Europe at the time considered private, not political. The Archbishop of Canterbury recently stated in the House of Lords that though no one had viewed with deeper repugnance the invasion of Ethiopia by Italy, he didn't know that any good purpose could be served by lamentations now. The headmaster of Rugby wants antiaircraft guns sent to anti-Fascist Spain because antiaircraft guns are not weapons of offense. Prime Minister Chamberlain has just declared that England will cease its "humane bombing" of rebels' houses in Iraq, Palestine, etc., since even humane bombing seems to offend Mr. Cordell Hull and a lot of men in Iraq, Palestine, etc. Though the name of Gladstone has long been associated with the old Liberal Party, and though the Liberal Party has long been associated with Free Trade, Lady Gladstone of today's Liberal Party has moved for an embargo on the shipment of oil to any aggressor country. Back in April, the secretary of the Non-Intervention Committee stated that France was the only major power which had paid its dues up to Christmas, that England would pay her back dues for October, November, and December if Germany and Italy paid theirs, and that unless somebody paid in close to half a million dollars pretty quickly, the Non-Intervention Committee would have to close up shop. Maybe it did temporarily and nobody noticed it. Lloyd's of London are made of sterner stuff than Mr. Chamberlain's government. They have just sent a bill of £250,000 to General Franco for the British ships sunk off Spain.

Obviously, European history now contains novelties. However, the queer fear that the British Prime Minister is pro-German is dying down. Certainly only a fool could suppose that a fly could be prospider, or that Chamberlain is a fly. What he is trying to do, aided by occasional prods from Lord Baldwin, by nudges from the Cabinet, by anxious pressure of public and Parliamentary opinion, is to discover which (provided England is given the choice) will prove the more costly—peace or war. Peace can cause a slump; it can also lead to the presence in Europe of a new empire—the *Grössere Deutschland*, stretching down from the Baltic and reaching out for the Black Sea. The truth is that none of the Mr. Chamberlains in the Continental countries know what concessions Herr Hitler will demand to keep the peace, or what little thing will make him go to war. The great and dangerous novelty in Europe today is indubitably the curious mind of Herr Hitler, a practical mystic whose unpredictable mental processes and moves, being unlike anything that the chancelleries have for centuries considered part of the game, have left diplomats foolishly standing ready with bats and no ball within reach. Because his mind is a type that Europe is unfamiliar with, for too long Europe complacently stated that Hitler had no mind at all. Europe is now having a chance to become familiar with it at a moment which, the democracies hope, is not too late.

Informed minds here seem to think there will be no war.

At Tooth's Gallery, Pavel Tchelitchew has had what amounts to a remarkable one-picture show with his canvas *Phenomena*. It required three years to paint, is nine by seven feet, and was damned in the *Sunday Times* and praised by the *Observer*. It is filled with dozens of figures, monsters and friends—portraits of Edith Sitwell, Cecil Beaton, Gertrude Stein, a bearded lady, a dog-faced boy, Mammon, skyscrapers, a prison, and other terrible or tenuous miracles of nature and modern life. Few painters today trouble to portray Hell; here is one painter's magnificently perspectived inferno, a superbly worked canvas whose fine composition cannot be denied, though its personal apocalyptic statement may well be argued. People are likely to be enormously moved or greatly repelled by *Phenomena*. Few could fail to see in the preliminary sketches—oddments of torsos, black-and-whites of heads, delicate silver points—the finest, the closest approach to great classical draughtsmanship attained by any young artist at work today. Tchelitchew's drawings are phenomena in themselves.

November 24

Though the approach, denouement, and aftermath of the Czechoslovakian crisis blacked out nearly half of London's October-November "little season," after-the-aftermath activity has made up for lost time. Traffic has been paralyzed four times in a fortnight—by the King and Queen's coach ride to the opening of Parliament; by the Lord Mayor's Show, which featured "national-fitness" bathing beauties; by the thankful crowds that attended this year's armistice ceremonies at the Cenotaph; and by the visit of King Carol and his heir, their landau drives through the city's gray streets, and their escorts, the chromatic Life and Coldstream Guards. The newspapers announced beneath photographs of the Rumanian King, "Cheers All the Way," and usually added (on another page) that he intended to ask the British government for a loan of £25,000,000.

English history consists of critical periods, of which this certainly is one. Unfortunately, history here has been taking things easy since the Munich

Accord. In England, as in France, that invaluable emotional momentum which arose when the Premier came home with peace in his pocket was allowed to lapse, leaving the people feeling lucky rather than secure. Now they don't even feel very lucky. The deficiencies in the arrangements for safeguarding the island's future—not only from sporadic bombs but also from continued proletarian poverty—are, at last, very grave matters indeed. What the public sensibly seeks is action, not talk, and it isn't getting much of either. After the opening of this crucial Parliamentary session, the kindest thing to be said for the King's do-less speech was that the King didn't write it. The Chamberlain government, which did, has since also hemmed about installing a Ministry of Supply and has hawed about compulsory national military service. Lord Castlerosse has said that what the House of Commons needs is members who are pro-British "and do not care a damn" for any other land. Anthony Eden has said that England can be first-rate or nothing, and will probably head a Central Left Coalition party to prove it—if mountainous Labour can bring forth anything but a mouse. The season's herring catch was a cruel disappointment; the barley crop brought the worst prices in years; lambs, another big English business, are being born a month too soon for the market. The newly hatched appeasement with Germany has overnight turned to a full-grown Frankenstein monster of horror and insults from Berlin; the *Times* no longer bellwethers public opinion; and Chamberlain, October's hero, will in January probably be reduced to hunting votes in a General Election. It is possible that the women of England, realistically happier in peace, for their men's sakes, than are Englishmen themselves, will keep him in power. Already he is a sort of national memento of a strange, unfought, and, in terms of slow time, possibly successful imperial battle to which England will raise no monument, since there were no dead.

General news is spotty. The cat-o'-nine-tails has been abolished in the excellent Penal Reform Bill of Sir Samuel Hoare, descendant of a prison reformer who unfortunately instituted treadmills. While Lord Snell, leader of the Opposition in the House of Lords, hopes that the King and Queen's visit to the States will "bring blessings not only to America and ourselves but to the world," many Americans here fear Their Majesties will find the blessings not unmixed. Owing to copyright control, "The Lambeth Walk" can't be sung (which means oi-oied) publicly except in the *Me and My Girl* show, which gave it birth. In a not distinguished London theatrical season, there is an outstanding new Central European actress—Wanda Rotha, now playing at the Garrick in *Elizabeth of Austria*.

A charity concert given at the Countess of Portarlington's house for the Greater London Fund for the Blind was a joy to the listeners' ears. The soiree featured a *causerie*, songs, and the accompanying of Reynaldo Hahn, that melodic, bewigged, talented Proustian figure once familiar in salons from Venice to the Thames, and now occasionally seen on the podium of the Opéra-Comique. He was the first of the modern French composers to set Verlaine to music, and was first in the tender musical memories of the Edwardian generation. Assembled to hear him in Belgravia, but attired and begemmed to go on to Buckingham Palace afterward for King Carol's ball, what is left of the Edwardians appeared to be full indeed of various memories.

Greeting the King and Queen, Neville Chamberlain, **Baldwin's successor, the "appeasement" Prime Minister. He gave the umbrella a bad name.**

Last summer it looked as if the next Salzburg were going to be either Versailles or Lucerne. Now it looks as if next year it's going to be Bath. Bath Arts Festival, Ltd., has just been founded with high hopes for the town's first season, from mid-July to mid-August, 1939, provided the local hostelries can be perked up in time to appeal to the carriage trade. The *festa* will start with a grand costume ball, to attract what Bath still calls "the world of fashion," and then settle down to rare orchestral and chamber music, with international stars singing and conducting, period plays produced by Tyrone Guthrie, of the Old Vic, and John Gielgud. To provide added entertainment, the old pagan baths have been metamorphosed into a swimming pool. As His Worship the Mayor told his Guildhall meeting, the festival will be the city's biggest chance in two thousand years. He referred to the town's Roman foundation and omitted its fabulous eighteenth-century gaiety, when its beaux, wit, gambling, and architecture made it the small talk of Europe. 131

With its pilastered terraces, its Pump and Assembly Rooms, Bath is still the most perfectly preserved piece of period city planning in the land. Fortunately for the festival folk, the Assembly Rooms have just been rehabilitated to the tune of £30,000 by an anonymous admirer, are now the property of the National Trust, and are rented to the town for a pound a year. With such a start, Bath's festivals should flourish.

NOVEMBER 30

Sobered by the September crisis, the early-winter season here has been carefully conservative in its music, its art, and its plays. Sibelius, old masters, and Marie Tempest have been the cautious mixture offered the public, with the Old Vic, the people's inexpensive delight, furnishing the sole experiment. At its worst the Old Vic is the liveliest theatre in London and at its best it is one of the few creative theatres in Europe today. The recent uncut version of *Hamlet*, in modern dress, was one of its finest productions. As for the modernity of the attire, to an American eye the Elsinore family, like most of official England today, looked very costumey indeed. Although the Ghost walked wearing a Tommy's tin hat, Hamlet had on rubber boots, and the mourners carried umbrellas to Ophelia's funeral, the King's regimentals were pure Ruritania, his retainers were decked out in scarlet mess kits, and the Court ladies were violently Victorian. The producer, Tyrone Guthrie, frankly and admirably aimed at melodrama, combining extreme stylization with up-to-date realism. During the play scene, the guests (as they would at any smart English castle today) chatted so loudly that the host and hostess could hardly hear themselves accused of murder. The duel scene, which contained the most dangerous and prolonged fencing we've ever seen on a stage, renovated and amplified the text. Alec Guinness was a sentient, fresh Hamlet—a tragic radical son who defiantly clothed himself in a sweater when his parents dressed for a Court dinner. As the final curtain speech stated, the Old Vic's *Hamlet* was much criticized, principally by people who didn't go to see it.

The annual Antique Dealers' Fair, which was recently held at Grosvenor House, was the best art show of the fortnight. Founded under the patronage of Queen Mary, that persistent collector, the Fair is a glorified Flea Market, displaying superb Georgian silver, break-front Chippendale bookcases, Waterford glass, Charles I sweetmeat dishes, fox-head stirrup cups, Wedgwood, Battersea enamel trifle boxes, and step-up Hepplewhite writing tables, untouched more than a hundred years. All the eccentricity and artisanship which gave English furnishings their shapes and styles were to be seen here. The Fair featured 108 stands chock-full of things made before 1830, including a Sheraton set of musical glasses, designed for parlor playing around 1790 and still sounding fine. Fashions in furniture are an important trade item in England. It would seem that eighteenth-century Chinese cabinets of lacquer, now mostly used to hold liquor, are again going out of style; that Queen Anne kneehole writing desks would be the new rage if there were enough to go around; and that the smartest English period furniture today is Regency, or what Americans could call President Madison.

It is considered here that Third Reich politics have reached the dangerous Pompadour period. Struggles for the power to influence Herr Hitler are now going on behind the Berlin scene, as similar ones once did behind the Bourbon throne. With all the chiefs of the European democracies reduced, since the Munich Accord, to functioning like handmaidens rather than like men of the world, the household loves and hates that shake the Nazi Party vibrate across the whole Continent.

It is supposed by some in London that Field Marshal Göring, who has always maneuvered to check Dr. Goebbels' activities, cruelly let the Doctor have his way with the pogroms in the hope that by overreaching himself he would fall and take his partner, Himmler, with him. Another explanation for the pogroms is that after the Paris Embassy murder, the Goebbels-Himmler combine suggested that Hitler might also be assassinated and, having thus built up fear, launched a pogrom as proof that they alone among his friends were safeguarding his life. There are wild rumors in high British circles that the Führer has indeed been shot at, that Goebbels has been whistled at in the streets, that his wife will divorce him, that the important avuncular affections of the Leader, hitherto centered on Goebbels' children, have switched to Göring's little daughter, that von Ribbentrop is playing a lone hand, that Hitler is ill, that the Reichswehr is dissatisfied, that the monarchy will be restored, that the Party will be purged—gossip ordinarily disdained by the pessimistic and sensible and now retailed with the nervousness of helplessness and hope. The strange psychology and physiology of the Nazi chiefs, their sublimations, deformities, hospital histories, and phobias, have finally alarmed political England to a degree which the degeneracy of its own kings never inspired.

In an effort to let Germany know what England says—even if England can't find out what Germany thinks—since the crisis the BBC has been putting on the air, every night at eight, in the German language, samples of British and world opinion and news, which must be news indeed to listening Germans and little like what their censors allow them.

Among country people, there's talk of returning, in the interests of direct government, to King and Council methods. It seems they worked well in the days of good Queen Bess. Among city people, the talk is only of America. Never, since our States were founded, has Europe looked toward us with more hope and envy. Ours seems to be the land of the free where men don't have to be brave.

DECEMBER 8

Apparently political crises are distinctly bad for the book trade here. The Abdication, the Coronation, the *Anschluss*, and the Munich Accord were all hard on the English reading-and-writing business, though book publishing was boomed by the 1914–1918 world war. However, the present season has produced several unexpected best-sellers, the chief one being Margaret Halsey's lively anti-English diary *With Malice Toward Some*, which the *Times Literary Supplement* solemnly listed under "sociology," as if Anglophobia were a new kind of distressed area. Margaret Lane's strange life of her stranger father-in-law, Edgar Wallace, is the Book Society's Christmas choice and will probably sell thirty thousand copies, a rare mark to reach here at any season. The Palestine muddle being what it is, David Garnett's *The Letters of T. E. Lawrence* has roused more than the usual Laurentian pro-and-con excitement. Bruce Lockhart's *Guns and Butter* is popular with minds which believe that journalists are historians. The costly *Complete Edition of Greville's Diaries*, unexpurgated at last (Queen Victoria had a fit even at their bowdlerized appearance in her lifetime), supplies the most expensive and expansive royal and political gossip since the Hanoverian dynasty was imported. Because Elizabeth Bowen is a writer's writer, the London Literati's fiction choice has been her *Death of the Heart*, which is less like a novel than like some pitiful street accident, at which one closes one's eyes, yet hears the thing happening to the victim. The tale is the tragedy of the first unfulfilled love and overfilled disillusion of a schoolgirl of sixteen, whose portrait, on many of the book's pages, is as clear to the vision as if the skillful Miss Bowen had painted, not written, it there. If you were ever sixteen, female, and in love, read this and weep.

The Sadler's Wells English ballet, or Vic-Wells Ballet, apparently revived in 1931 so that balletomanes could compare it unfavorably with Diaghilev's Russian Ballet of 1914, has now ceased to function on that basis and has become an admirably adept and handsome young local troupe, artistically alive and kicking rhythmically twice weekly, nine months in the year, at popular prices. While it still gets into hot water when it attempts to emulate the fussy foreign tradition, it furnishes enchanting distraction when it performs its own creations, of which to date six at least are choreographically, musically, or decoratively of importance. These are *The Rake's Progress*, after Hogarth's pictures; *Nocturne*, with music by Delius; *Les Patineurs*, an operatic skating ballet; *Apparitions*, with music by Liszt, and choreography and an emotional theme so importantly new that it was immediately copied by the Russians in their *Boutique Fantasque*; *Checkmate*, with costumes and curtains by London's master poster artist, E. McKnight Kauffer, which rank ocularly with the best of Diaghilev's postwar novelties; and finally *Horoscope*, which has zestful music by Constant Lambert. Lambert, the orchestra leader; the ballet mistress, Ninette de Valois, former *ballerina assoluta;* and Frederick Ashton, the choreographer, have developed the ballet to the point where it prettily pirouettes today. Technically, the dancing of Helpmann, of the delicate, deft Margot Fonteyn, of the Toumanova-like June Brae, and of Pamela May is a delight. The Sadler's Wells ballet is still a neighborhood affair, patronized by some snobs but mostly by poorish people from just around the corner and by balletomane charladies who clap like mad and without criticism. This is bad for the ballet. It is also good for the ballet. It made possible its success.

Art has been varied. There has been a rich from-El-Greco-through-Goya exhibition for the relief of Spain. Tooth's Gallery has shown Epstein's new illustrations for Baudelaire's *Fleurs du Mal*, which would surprise the poet and astonish the floral kingdom. The Leicester has displayed Disney's original drawings for *Snow White* and a first exhibition of paintings by Oliver Messel. He seems to be several Messels, judging from the variety of his styles—four heads of Tilly Losch, all on one canvas and as sensuously strong as a fresco; one head of Princess Natalie Paley (Mrs. Jack Wilson), in a Lalique glass-green manner; and some absolutely elegant French Impressionist brushwork and really good oil painting, as in *Lady Mendl's Party at Versailles* and the artist's décor for *Midsummer Night's Dream*. Messel's likenesses, such as the portraits of Lady Elizabeth Paget, Jimmy Daniels, and the Princess K. de Kapurthala, are gifts his generation should preserve.

Not in fifty years, Winston Churchill has stated, have there been such bitter cleavages in people's political opinions. Friends fall out and lovers quarrel over the Munich appeasement; family ties are strained by Grandmother's threatening to vote Labour in spite of her pro-Chamberlain spouse. It's good that somebody shows some activity. The government shows none. It seems to be in that state, awake, in which individuals find themselves in dreams—a nightmare of running without arrival. A population which expressed gratitude at having been saved from September's war would now be grateful to know what it will do in next spring's or another autumn's battles, when, judging by the present lack of organization, the Englishman's umbrella is going to be his best bomb protection, unless he prefers the fox-hole trenches that still disfigure London's parks. There is no department of private or political life where lack of surety in planning, absence of talent and time sense, and the presence of that gift for courageous muddle that is so endearing to the English do not now evidence themselves, at least in the public's estimation. Indeed, the only excellent traditional qualities still manifest are patience and dignified belief. Unfortunately these are not confined to the man in the street, where they belong, but also mark the gentlemen sitting in Parliament—at a moment when only urgency and skepticism will refresh a body politic whose fatigue is now tiring the democratic Europe it once so remarkably invigorated.

1939 The weather and the grand opera that annually open the London May season are usually considered of great importance here. The season has just got under way with *The Bartered Bride* and two days of rain instead of the customary seventeen-day deluge. While the weather has bettered this year, Covent Garden's opera has not. There have been half-filled houses for a half-hearted series of productions which nearly didn't get under way and might as well not have bothered to, since in London, this spring, opera is not what matters.

The important drama here at the moment is that played by the great public and the Chamberlain government. Since a general election would be an act of national frivolity at such a grave time, Mr. Chamberlain remains in Downing Street, but it cannot be inferred that public confidence entirely dwells there with him. Because of what he did at Munich in September, millions of English sincerely clung to him. Because of what Herr Hitler did at Prague in March, a multitude of English have pulled away from their Premier and his policy. It's common talk that never before in modern parliamentary times have the government and the country been so separated, with so little chance either of getting together or of getting rid of each other. The thinking aristocrats feel the Premier has showed a middle-class, mercantile mind, devoid of the *savoir-faire* needed in diplomatic battles and unequipped with any proud notion of British prestige, which in times past has sometimes saved face though the battle was lost. The moneyed middle class doesn't mind his mercantile mind but deplores his having made bad bargains and bought Hitlerian shoddy that any clever merchant—on second glance, anyhow—should have seen wouldn't wear. While the industrial middle class still contains many of his die-hard supporters, who truly figure that peace hurts trade less than war, the bulk of passionate pro-Chamberlainites are now the old people, tenderly anxious about their grandsons and wisely fearful of the ferocities of a fight. What the vast unmoneyed, unaristocratic British public resents in Chamberlain is his having picked for his ministers inefficient, dawdling yes-men, tragically unsuited to a time when "No" may be the decisive word and when speedy efficacy must be the very life breath of the nation.

With what the government does and what the people think being separate affairs, for the first time in generations English newspapers are not molding public opinion but are being led by it. Those papers which have failed to follow it have lost authority, or readers, or both. Thus the mighty *Times* has sunk to second place in sticking by the government, for which, if it dares not thunder, at any rate it can occasionally noisily drop an official brick, like the recent "Danzig is not really worth a war." The leading powerful daily is now the *Telegraph*, which is anti-Downing Street, anti-Nazi, pro-Halifax, pro-Foreign office. Because of their unpopular isolationist policy, Lord Beaverbrook's *Standard* and gay, American-mannered *Express* both have lost heavily in circulation, it is said, even though the *Express* was shrill against the Premier, acid about his ministers, and compassionate for the poor farmer and his unploughed lands. Lord Rothermere's pro-Nazi memoirs having been published at the same time as news of the fall of Prague, his *Daily*

William Maxwell Aitken,
Lord Beaverbrook.

Mail, to appease the public, has climbed down somewhat out of the fifth
Column, as the pro-German group is called here. The mysterious morning
Mirror (no one seems sure who owns it) has flourished on its blunt anti-
government editorials, initialed "W.M." Of the special feature writers, those
most eagerly read have been Winston Churchill and the more careful Alfred
Duff Cooper, who, with Anthony Eden, Harold Nicolson, and R. S. Hud-
son, should (or so many people, not, apparently, including the five gentlemen themselves, think) put new, rebellious blood into the old Conservative
Party. The *Manchester Guardian* remains the illuminating intelligentsia
guide; the weekly *New Statesman* still strongly sticks up for the feeble
Labour Party and its anticonscription stand. The liveliest acrobatics have
been those of the Sunday *Observer's* elderly editorialist J. L. Garvin, who,
after having been anti-Russian and pro-German for twenty years, became
pro-Russian and anti-German in a single septuagenarian somersault as amazing for its agility as for its literary style.

While Chamberlain may not be following the policy the public wants,
it is known that he is now following a policy he doesn't want, either. No one
can know what this will really come to until everyone is positive what Russia
has done with Litvinov and what Beck intends to do with Poland.

Some people's business here in London is fine; other people's business is
awful. Money does not flow when few feel optimistic. Like all nervous
European cities, London is throwing its energy into snack bars, cinemas,
any sort of pastime. The four entertainment sellouts in town have been Toscanini's seven Beethoven Queen's Hall concerts; the American film of *Wuth-
ering Heights*; Clare Boothe's *The Women*, which the Censor hoped would
be called *The American Women*, so no one could think the characters were
English ladies; and Lord Berners' and Sir Francis Rose's new Sadler's Wells   137

Anton Walbrook, Diana Wynyard, and Rex Harrison in *Design for Living*.

Of the three great European theatre centers in the 1930s—London, Berlin, Paris—it was that of London which outshone and outtalked them all. A creative, critical faculty animated the London stage, exemplified by the ribald exuberance of its revues and Shakespearean productions and the timeless polished performances, shining with wit and malice, in its up-to-date, traditional comedies.

Mischievous, mocking choir boy or scathing female commentator. Either way, one of the funniest stage wits we have ever seen—Beatrice Lillie, "Weary of It All" (Noël Coward's lyrics), surrounded by Robert Eddison, Tony Hulley, and Hugh French in *All Clear*.

Noël Coward and Gertrude Lawrence in *Tonight at 8:30.*
Stage children, doomed to come to a bad end, and they just turned
into stars, that's all. My word, what good fun they gave us. How
secure they made our theatrical pleasures. No worry about *that* show
if *they* were in it.

ballet, *Cupid and Psyche*, based on a chapter in Walter Pater's *Marius the Epicurean*. Berners' music was what ballet music ought to be—melodic, gay, impulsively rhythmic, written for dancers' feet rather than for critics' ears. The Frederick Ashton choreography was of an inventively patterned grace that brought to mind the old fertile Russian days and introduced a slim seventeen-year-old dancing star, Julia Farron. Sir Francis Rose's meticulously painted décor was Sino-Greco, his costume colors broadly Hellenic; both were welded in an eclectic vision that London hailed as a triumph. Sir Francis has become one of the theatre's important new designers. The première of *Cupid and Psyche* was notable for twenty curtain calls and a slight shindig in the gallery when Leftist balletomanes thought that the dancing Jupiter and Juno were miming the Fascist salute. Even pirouettes look political these days.

MAY 17

To anybody lucky enough not to be able to read, London would seem to be the same as usual. It is the grave headlines in the newspapers that establish a difference, and above all the printed calls for volunteers on the city's buses, billboards, and public monuments. A stone's throw from Hyde Park's pacifist soapbox orators, the Marble Arch is draped with a great banner which cries, "Be Prepared! National Service! Have You Offered Yours?" In Piccadilly Circus, the famous statue of Eros, god of Love, now lifts his wings above billboards declaring, "We've Got to Be Prepared." Among the symbolic British lions in Trafalgar Square, the Air Ministry has placed a recruiting slogan: "England Expects That YOU Will Enroll Today." In the Green Park, beneath the windows of the Ritz, are signs left over from last September, still stating "These Trenches Are Dangerous," which everyone hopes they no longer are, since they must serve as the principal air-raid shelter for all Mayfair. In the drive-yourself automobiles for hire is the warning, "In the outbreak of hostilities this car is requisitioned for the Air Raid Precautions Services. You are requested to bring it back at the earliest possible convenience."

If hostilities do break out, many functioning units of London are going to be moved early, with probable inconvenience. It's already planned that the government will shift to Bath; the Stock Exchange will go to Oxford; London University will go to Liverpool; the Law Courts will sit "somewhere out of London," with wartime juries of seven men instead of twelve; Guy's Hospital will be transferred to Farnham; the choicest pictures in the National Gallery will, as they were during the autumn crisis, be taken somewhere in Wales, traveling, as if they were precious people, in a special train. Evacuation of London's population is also planned by air-bombardment experts, who oddly state that "the best treatment is that which accepts the necessity of a proportion of casualties, but arranges that they should fall only on those who cannot be evacuated." In Lambeth (home of the Walk), nine thousand citizens with modest incomes were offered free Anderson backyard air-raid-shelter cabins and three thousand refused to accept them, because they thought them deathtraps, and anyway the cabins would ruin their newly planted gardens. London citizens with an annual income of over

Trafalgar Square.

£250 don't have to worry about their gardens, since free shelters aren't offered them.

Though the Territorial Anti-Aircraft and Field Force still needs nearly two hundred thousand men to make up that volunteer army which the Labour party said could "provide all the man power required for security against aggression," protests against conscription continue; proconscriptionist complaints, usually about the slowness of the government, are even livelier. If the Conscription Bill passes its third reading in Parliament, England's conscription will start on June 30, when fifty thousand young men will be called up; the last of the projected two hundred thousand conscripts will finish their military training in July 1940, if Herr Hitler doesn't mind waiting for the enemy till then. Chamberlain has just assured Free Church leaders that sympathy will be shown their members who are conscientious objectors (apparently adherents to the Established or Episcopalian Church are entitled neither to conscience nor to objections). The Methodists of Richmond have declared, "War is contrary to the purpose of our Lord;" Presbyterians seem of two minds about this. The powerful Manchester Quakers state that compulsory military service prevents the individual from "following the leadings of the spirit of God within him." The Labour party thinks wealth should be conscripted before men are. The Cambridge Union debated on and decided against conscription; the Oxford Union debated on and decided for conscription.

Since, as the wits honestly state, the country is not behind the government but ahead of it, and since for months everybody except the government realized that conscription would probably come, talk against it is largely to demonstrate the great English right of free speech and of doing unaccustomed things very slowly, if at all—both national tenets Britons still proudly indulge in. There hasn't been a peacetime conscripted army here since the days of Oliver Cromwell's General Monck. The Nazis may operate with lightning speed over weekends. The English are still moving with all their traditional majesty.

Davis Cup elimination matches have started at the Sussex County Lawn Tennis Club. Bombing planes of the RAF have been making daylight demonstration flights over Surrey, Berkshire, and Hampshire. Though likenesses of the peerage abounded at the Royal Academy's exhibition, the only hit portrait was of a former circus fat lady who sideshowed under the name of Trixie. Léon Blum, who was designated by the French government to come over and talk (through a translator) to the British Labour Party if it started to practice what it preached against conscription, has come here to talk to Labour anyhow. The new high taxes for armament include a soaking of the newsreels, during the past year the government's unpaid, faithful propaganda servant. In the new and ugly Waterloo Bridge, which replaced the handsome old one, a cylinder has been placed for posterity's enlightenment—should this bridge ever be destroyed to make way for one uglier still. The cylinder contains copies of the *Times*, *Telegraph*, Leftist *Herald*, etc., with their reports on Herr Hitler's seizure of Memel, plus copies of *Vogue* and the *Tailor & Cutter*, with their reports on what Paris and London were wearing when Memel was seized.

While London thinks that things look calmer, there is still anxious curiosity about the future. In an effort to satisfy it, the city's horoscope devotees have been consulting the stars. Thus on May 11, eager to know if

RAF planes overhead.

Stalin would sign the Anglo-Russian pact, the public read in the *Express*, "Children born today will be very clever, be deep thinkers, and possess a logical, well-balanced intellect. Today is the birthday of Irving Berlin."

MAY 23

Though the Sunday *Times* feared that "one of the most punishing winters within memory, an unusually cold spring, and a long period of political unrest" would affect the Chelsea Flower Show, it was as resplendent as ever. This is the greatest floral tent show on earth. It is no place for a writer, or even a painter; only the Chelsea flowers can properly speak for themselves or paint their own amazing colors. The show lasts three days, the first being reserved for visits by royalty, officialdom, and the Royal Horticultural Society's thirty-seven thousand members. The best time to see it is the afternoon before it opens to anyone except humble, aproned gardeners, laying the last-minute carpets of moss beneath begonias as pink and fragile as camellias and as large as cabbages, unwrapping cotton from giant lilium-auratum stamens, or packing the peat around purple gloxinias that look like clusters of Royal Worcester teacups. As usual, the most dramatic and beautiful single item in the show was the seed merchant Sutton's annual set piece, a hundred feet square and composed entirely of blooms. This year's was a landscape with a forest made of all shades of salpiglossis; waterfalls of blue lobelia; lakes of pale-blue petunias; plains of violet antirrhinum, orange African ursinia, pale mallow, and sweet-scented stock; and little lowlands of brilliant nemesia. It takes Sutton's men two days to build this *tableau vivant* and wire or pat each of the thousands of potted plants into place. In general, the Chelsea Show seemed to indicate that if orchids, amaryllis, and flame-toned azaleas are holding their own, rock gardens are fading in popularity; that nothing has taken the place of the blue poppy as a floral shock; and that auricula, which, as "dusty millers," had an inexplicable popularity with Manchester cotton spinners around 1860, are coming back into style. Tulips also were popular this year, since the show, which is usually too late for them, was held a week early so as not to conflict with Derby Day. It isn't often that race horses give tulips a break.

Ever since the last war, the poor have been assured by their political leaders that war is the rich man's gold mine, out of which he makes new millions. As a plutocrat's investment, the next war shapes up doubtfully, judging by the way European stock markets sag every crisis week. Indeed, the only old-style gilt-edged investment in London today would seem to be the baby giant panda, Ming, at the Regent's Park Zoo. She (though maybe she is he; the Zoo isn't sure) cost £1,000 and has already earned £15,000, or a nice 1400 per cent, for the Zoological Society. She has been the greatest moneymaker the Zoo has ever known. In 1850, the first hippopotamus to reach Europe since the days of ancient Rome was displayed at Regent's Park; his name was Obaysch, people lined the railway tracks just to see him arrive, and 360,402 citizens paid to see him at closer quarters during what was called Hippopotamus Year. The chimpanzee Jubilee drew a good gate, too, but she never touched Ming, who in Easter week pulled in eighteen thousand more visitors than the Zoo got during the last and panda-less holy season.

Since Ming's arrival, on Christmas Eve, she has attracted three hundred thousand customers. Ming has also been a riot in the wholesale and retail trades. London is swamped with pandas in soap, on brooches, buttons, chintz, and nursery wallpaper, and in children's picture books, of which the nicest is Sheila Hawkins' *The Panda and the Piccaninny*. It's no *Ferdinand*, but it's certainly the finest two-minute novel about a panda we ever read. Unofficial reports state that when Queen Mary went to the Zoo to visit Ming, the more the frisky panda advanced, the more the Queen retreated, with dignity. Ming also recently met Winston Churchill. They got along fine.

Since the young King and Queen, by sailing on the *Empress of Australia*, automatically changed the ship pro tem from a mere commercial liner into a royal yacht under Admiralty command, there has been no official criticism of, though there has been a lot of private comment on, Their Majesties' icebound voyage. As had been patiently expected, their being in North America has taken the impetus away from a none-too-animated social season, and tradesmen as a result are suffering more than debutantes. Some of these young ladies are making their coming-out bow in their ancestral country mansions, for many families, alarmed by the September crisis into extended rustication, have during the succeeding crises remained in the country and left their Belgravia town houses unopened. London business has sickened. Nor is its convalescence anywhere near being in sight. If this is already the war that we're living in—this disruption of European men's earning their cake and bread; this unbroken semimobilization of fleet or army now obtaining in England, France, Poland, Switzerland, Holland, Spain, Belgium, Germany, and Italy; this unhealthy armament budget, which taxes all men to death; and this constant commerce in arms, while peaceable manufacturing perishes—if these things are, as some think, the new or "white" war, and all the war there's ever going to be, then mankind is fortunate, no matter how soon it sinks into the coma of bankruptcy. The political and financial practices of England and France, as capitalistic democracies, are fairly old. There's a strong feeling that, apart from the weight, in terms of human masses, which Russia could bring to an alliance, some modern element is a necessity on the Allied side to balance that contemporary quality in Nazism which may be its greatest single strength. The British Institute of Public Opinion, patterned after Dr. Gallup's polls and little considered here because of its Leftist hopes, reports 87 per cent of a cross-section of English opinion in favor of the Russian alliance.

That some sort of modernism will have to mar England's elderly surface shapeliness seems inevitable. Had the Russians been as efficient as the Germans, their revolution would have had some practical imitation even here. What with the emotional Russian Revolution of 1917 and the systematic German Revolution of 1933, pressure is finally accumulating which will force new methods, if not doctrines, on European countries which, even while avoiding Communism and Fascism, are now in a slow process of becoming something different from what they once were. And no diplomatic umbrella will stave off this change.

Overleaf: One of the largest recruiting drives in London, organized by the auxiliary fire service.

For the moment, it would seem as if contemporary European history could be used as the libretto of a comic opera. After a solemn preliminary diplomatic announcement by Señor Pierre Leao Velloso, new Brazilian Ambassador to Rome, that his government was studying a plan to relieve Italy's grave coffee shortage, the Genoa Football Club announced that a player named Figliola had been traded to the Rio de Janeiro club for four hundred and sixteen bags of coffee. Owing to the nervousness in provincial England over the Irish Republican bomb outrages, Mr. Alfred Hockley, landlord of the Vinols Cross Inn at West Hoathly, alarmed by a customer's package that emitted a buzzing sound, courageously tossed out of the bar window what proved to be the customer's new hive of bees. Because of the uncertainty of the international money market, Swiss banks are buying Cézannes, which they consider less unreliable than gold. Objection by poor London mothers to the government's air-raid evacuation plans has been so solid that evacuation is now being presented as optional, not compulsory. The Derby was run in what the papers termed a heat wave and what the thermometer registered as exactly a comfortable 74°. Germany has announced that England's general election will take place next September. The College of Heralds has worked out a new relationship for the King and President Roosevelt; they meet at Washington not only as guest and host but also as cousins. It seems they're both descended from William the Conqueror via Henry II—the King through Edward II, the President through Henry the Lion, Duke of Saxony. The Heralds also have linked George Washington to both, through Henry II. It's just one big democratic family. As soon as the Russian treaty is fixed up, the Chamberlain government is going to be in hot water again in Parliament. There will be questions about the allegedly disastrous cleaning of the Elgin Marbles, for apparently somebody washed all the antique patina off.

England is getting on with her preparations for war. At the Duke of York's Headquarters near the Chelsea Hospital's gardens, young civilians in tweeds or work clothes can be seen at their Saturday-afternoon voluntary drill. Airplane factories, though bothered by bureaucracy's blatherskiting, are turning out planes at a rate which, experts swear, Germany cannot keep up with, as Germany well knows. The experts also say that inflation is paying for all this, and that later, whether there has been a war or not, there will be a slump which will mow down the industrial battalions as if by the very weapons they've been manufacturing. The women are working like nailers. According to Miss Ellen Wilkinson, Socialist M.P. for Jarrow, the Women's Army is being run by society cliques. Yet the head of all the Women's Voluntary Services for Civil Defence is the Dowager Marchioness of Reading. She is a former justice of the peace, was a tireless welfare worker during the black days when babies in the depressed areas were being clothed in newspapers, and is an unerratic, businesslike organizer. Mrs. Montagu Norman, wife of the head of the Bank of England, is organizing the W.A.T.S. (Women's Auxiliary Territorial Service) for the north. The Women's Institutes, a determined group already represented in nearly every village on the island, are coöperating with the Army in making billeting plans. Already there are fifteen thousand volunteers for whole or part-time war work—as ambulance drivers, in the women's land army, doing odd jobs, handling communications (which means anything, from riding a motorbike to driving a six-wheeled truck), as air-raid wardens, as first-aid experts, with the Red Cross, with the St. John Ambulance Corps, as nurses, or as firemen. This last group seems a popular unit, with its smart blue red-trimmed uniforms. Lots of them are already visible at ladies' luncheon tables.

The Germans are organizing, too, though one reads nothing about it in the papers. After Easter, a quarter of a million German women between the ages of fourteen and twenty-five started their *Pflichtjahr* of domestic or agricultural service. Critics say it is the latest Nazi device to combine state service and love of the soil. It also is a partial solution of the pressing economic problem. The Duty Year will, in general, send country girls (if not married) to town as domestics and will send city girls of all classes to the country to milk cows, tend flocks, and clean floors or babies on peasant farms where there is a shortage of labor. This is the severest dose of democracy that history has ever seen; it could, indeed, only be put over by an autocracy.

Many people in London say there will be war in six weeks, or in six months, or not at all. That's more choice than we've been used to.

JUNE 8

Italy's taking Albania ruined the English Easter holiday. No one, fortunately, took anything during Whitsuntide—except the millions of Londoners who took from Friday to Tuesday off and had the sunniest, least politically clouded Bank Holiday of the year. Parliament, making a nice distinction between a state of ease and one of alarm, donated to itself a nine-day vacation rather than the ten days customary when Europe is behaving itself.

Over the holiday, thousands of Londoners and visitors went to the greyhound tracks. There are eight of them here, the topnotchers being Harringay, Stamford Bridge, and White City, which had a sixteen-race night program on Whitmonday. Britons being born bettors, the wagering is terrific, both with the tote and the bookies, who stand by the betting machines—which look as if they might sell chewing gum—and always wear smart light gloves in order to wave signals to their odds-getters across the track. Bets start at two shillings, the favorite wagers being a "forecast," which means picking the first two dogs to finish. The payoff on such a bet ranges from around thirty-five shillings to five or even eight pounds—with luck. White City is prettier by night than the Paris track, if only because the English turf is more beautifully green. It also is more formal. When the attendants of the dogs parade the animals around the track before each race, they march in step and swing their arms like Grenadiers; they wear high black boots, long white coats, and straw hats if it's a regular race, derbies if it's a trophy event. After the race, the attendants of the three winning hounds line up before the grandstand under a spotlight and in triumphant unison tip their three straw hats or three derbies, as the case may be. It's very impressive.

This year's much advertised London Music Festival has principally consisted of listing as part of the Festival all the concerts and recitals booked in former years as ordinary concerts and recitals. However, there have been important changes, for chamber music by the Royal Philharmonic Society was given for the first time in the great gallery of the Wallace Collection at Hertford House, a magnificent setting for Pergolesi and the Brandenburg Concerto. Even more popular still was an outdoor nocturnal brass-band performance of Handel's *Fireworks Music* and *Water Music* in the natural amphitheater of Ken Wood, near Hampstead Heath. Loudspeakers were set up among the bushes, families picnicked from lunch baskets, lovers lolled on the grass, the brasses sounded fairly fine, cannons were shot off to punctuate the tunes as Handel intended, and the fireworks were superb. The pyrotechnic set piece of a cockfight was literally a bird, with pinwheel feathers a-flying and radiating beauty and a welcoming look of warmth, since the night was chill.

At first it was thought that the Crisis was still hurting books. Now it has been ascertained that it's the nightly nine-o'clock BBC radio news bulletin (usually about other crises, it's true) which has done after-dinner book-reading in. If a family is alone, it sits around afterward, jawing about the news till bedtime, and if guests are present everyone argues about Hitler and Mussolini till midnight. In any case, those two men have encircled the British book trade.

Though "best-seller" is thus a relative term, the following volumes are, in their class anyhow, the most important London reading matter now: In fiction, *A Family and a Fortune,* by Miss I. Compton-Burnett. Like all this elderly authoress's garrulous, acid, polite, funny, shrewd half-dozen novels (today a cult in Bloomsbury), this is 1900 English middle-class lithography, a bit drab in color and complicated in character for American eyes. Among biographies, Lord David Cecil's *The Young Melbourne,* a masterpiece that resuscitates the period and Victoria's old adviser, and once again slays sad, mad, bad young Lady Caroline Lamb. In philosophy, *The Philosophical Fragments* and *Fear and Trembling,* by Sören Kierkegaard—Danish anti-materialist, contemporary of Hans Christian Andersen, and the prototype of Ibsen's Brand—who is now having some quiet emotional influence here. Among dramas, G. B. Shaw's *Geneva,* as disrespectful about the League as you'd hope and suspect, and illustrated by the spirited drawings of Feliks Topolski. Unfortunately, it doesn't include his brilliant portrait of the author. Foreign-situation books by journalists are as numerous as the Elsie Dinsmore books and equally sad. The three just out are John Gunther's *Inside Asia*, Oriental twin to his still fabulously popular *Inside Europe; France and Munich*, by the *Manchester Guardian*'s Paris correspondent, Alexander Werth, the first book to treat France lucidly and logically as a new second-rate power of importance; and, thirdly, *The Eleventh Hour,* Vincent Sheean's eagerly awaited volume. This opens with an anti-London chapter, which is bound to give the British fits, and moves on to Sheean's concentrated personal history during the last nine months in Spain, Austria, Czechia, and the more ideal and intelligent Europe inside his own mind. As for

Sir Winston Churchill—**not only a great personage but one of the few great personalities of his time.**

poetry, there's *Death of a Bull Fighter*, by Federico García Lorca, one of the best and least political poets of Europe, who was unhappily shot by Fascists. This is rare new verse admirably translated from the original Spanish by Stephen Spender.

An opus not yet off the press, but much looked forward to in Mayfair, is *My Royal Past, As Told to Cecil Beaton*. It's an extremely funny and sad life history, illustrated with Beaton photographs, of a mythical prewar baroness.

All these are the surface of London—books, races, holidays. The surface is where a city must live in times of suspense, unless the people desire to go mad. No one does here. London is sensibly super-sane.

JUNE 15

AMONG people who think twice, all this quiet on Europe's western front is alarming. Only a comfortable ninny could think the war of 1938–1939 is over now just because nothing is happening. The past year's worry as to what Herr Hitler would do next has been succeeded by this month's anxiety as to why he doesn't do anything at all. He still has considerable choice. Danzig would vote "*Ja*" for him even though the Polish government, formerly pro-Nazi, has turned anti-German along with its people; he can still end the autonomy of sullen Slovakia; but the real goal of his aims is even farther to the east, and it is one which England eventually will try to keep him from reaching—the Dardanelles, where the humanists, so-called, may fight the Huns for the trade route out to the Orient. Probably the worst psychological move in Hitler's campaign so far was Signor Mussolini's capture of Albania. By seizing it on Good Friday, Italy not only temporarily scandalized the Church but, what was more grave, aroused the Mohammedan world in anger against the Axis. If the big war really comes (and Hitler has declared that he's against it), it may see the Crusaders (now British Episcopalians and French neo-Thomists) again on the Golden Horn, fighting on the side of the infidels against the new heathen Brown Shirts from Berlin. Maybe the polite appeasers and the sterner preparers who know that the Allies can't be ready until next year will till then let things slide—into Hitler's pockets. as usual. But he cannot wait long; being poor, Germany must hurry. Being rich, England can afford to wait. In any case, prophets here think that the Mediterranean will be the scene of battle. Because Germany is best in the air, England, who is best at sea, must focus on fighting with ships, and Italy's several weaknesses, moral and material, add to the local attractions.

Indeed, there is so much practical planning for this next war, so much conversation about it, such explicit discussion in the morning papers, such earnest open muddling, such irony in the Czech's having begged for protection and in the Esthonians' having refused it, such farce in Russia's sniffing at what she once would have swallowed whole, such unconscious gaiety in British officials' losing state papers in sinister taxicabs, such humor in Parliament's having given only one day to debate on the affairs of the great British Colonial Empire—there is so much which is strange in all this that maybe Hitler's having a vast army just so he won't ever have to use it is no queerer than anything else going on in Europe today.

Sometimes things sound so crazy that one can't believe they apply to this world. It must be a couple of other planets.

Mrs. Roosevelt's "My Royal Guests" column in the *Standard* caused confusion, excitement, and wonder. To honor "the historic occasion" when the British sovereigns first set foot on what is now United States soil, the *Times* issued on June 8 a special supplement, with articles about America's Constitution, its governmental system, and the New Deal, all written from the British historical standpoint, very strange and interesting to American eyes. There's considerable relief in the American colony that the inevitable New World shout of "Hyah, King!" came first from a Canadian. There's relief, too, on the part of the British public, the Palace circle, and the press that the visit aroused "a popular demonstration beyond expectations," with the Queen and her smile (the public was betting on both) proving to be the big hit.

London's recent heat wave registered 85° in Hyde Park, where a lady's hat caught fire, kindled by the sun's rays on her bonnet's glass ornament. Visitors tend to think that Londoners would love it if their climate were better. After a fortnight of blue skies, the English moaned for some nice, familiar bad weather. England's soil is thin, water rates are high, without frequent drizzles delphiniums and hay perish alike. In the boiling heat, Britain's first conscripted peacetime army received its initial instructions about making war. Great Britain, incidentally, is only a little larger than Utah, but nearly 80 per cent of the Empire's soldiers killed in the last war came from these islands.

Because of the glare from London's lights, the great Greenwich Observatory, where Greenwich time comes from, must move. In many ways here, time marches on.

The Westminster Clock, counting the hours before . . .

Photo Acknowledgments

The author and the publishers wish to thank the following for their kind permission to reproduce the photographs which appear on the pages noted: Cecil Beaton, 83, 98, 151; Angus McBean Photograph, Harvard Theatre Collection, 14 top, 15, 40, 89, 123, 124 bottom, 125, 138; Horst, 9 right, 53, 95 (photo by Hoyningen-Huene), 119; Mme. Tussaud's Wax Museum, 66; The New York Public Library at Lincoln Center, Astor, Lenox and Tilden Foundations: Dance Collection, 85, 94, Theatre Collection, 14 left, 19, 41, 124 top, 139; Radio Times Hulton Picture Library, 15, 51, 52 top left and right, 58, 60, 73, 115, 137; Rolls-Royce Ltd., 45; United Press International, 8, 9 left. All other photographs come from the European Picture Service.

Index

Page numbers in italics indicate illustrations.

157